BRINGING BACK OUR
FRESHWATER
LAKES

BY LISA J. AMSTUTZ

CONTENT CONSULTANT

Dr. Gary Lamberti
Professor of Biological Sciences and
Director, Stream and Wetland
Ecology Laboratory
University of Notre Dame

Essential Library
An Imprint of Abdo Publishing
abdopublishing.com

CONSERVATION
SUCCESS STORIES

abdopublishing.com

Published by Abdo Publishing, a division of ABDO, PO Box 398166, Minneapolis, Minnesota 55439. Copyright © 2018 by Abdo Consulting Group, Inc. International copyrights reserved in all countries. No part of this book may be reproduced in any form without written permission from the publisher. Essential Library™ is a trademark and logo of Abdo Publishing.

Printed in the United States of America, North Mankato, Minnesota
092017
012018

Cover Photo: Guenter Guni/iStockphoto
Interior Photos: Bettman/Getty Images, 4; AP Images, 6; Tony Dejak/AP Images, 10–11; Steven Russell Smith Photos/Shutterstock Images, 12; iStockphoto, 14, 29, 45, 47, 48, 54, 79, 82, 98 (bottom right), 99 (left); Europics/Newscom, 16, 98 (middle left); Michael B. Watkins/iStockphoto, 18; Heike Kampe/iStockphoto, 20; Anne Kitzman/Shutterstock Images, 23; Dan Lewis/Shutterstock Images, 26; Shutterstock Images, 28, 33, 51, 61, 98 (top right); Dietmar Temps/Shutterstock Images, 30–31; Otto Stadler ImageBroker/Newscom, 32; Mark Edwards/UIG/Science Source, 35; Red Line Editorial, 36, 66; Tristan Tan/Shutterstock Images, 37; Nathan Hobbs/iStockphoto, 41; Jim West/ImageBroker/Glow Images, 42; Greg Vaughn/Alamy, 56; Jeffrey M. Frank/Shutterstock Images, 59; Olivier Le Queinec/Shutterstock Images, 60; Marcelo Horn/iStockphoto, 62, 98 (top left); John M. Burnley/Science Source, 65; Filipe Frazao/Shutterstock Images, 68; Merkushev Vasiliy/Shutterstock Images, 70–71; Simon Bradfield/iStockphoto, 72, 99 (right); L. Pettet/iStockphoto, 78; Jason Lindsey/Alamy, 80, 98 (bottom left); Jeff Caughey/Shutterstock Images, 84; Mike Haring/iStockphoto, 87; Carlos Osorio/AP Images, 88; Portland Press Herald/Getty Images, 90–91; Sabena Jane Blackbird/Alamy, 94–95; Tom McHugh/Science Source, 96; Tom Uhlman/Alamy, 97

Editor: Claire Mathiowetz
Series Designer: Laura Polzin

Publisher's Cataloging-in-Publication Data

Names: Amstutz, Lisa J., author.
Title: Bringing back our freshwater lakes / by Lisa J. Amstutz.
Description: Minneapolis, Minnesota : Abdo Publishing, 2018. | Series: Conservation success stories | Includes online resources and index.
Identifiers: LCCN 2017946774 | ISBN 9781532113147 (lib.bdg.) | ISBN 9781532152023 (ebook)
Subjects: LCSH: Lake conservation--Juvenile literature. | Restoration ecology--Juvenile literature. | Conservation of natural resources--Juvenile literature.
Classification: DDC 333.911--dc23
LC record available at https://lccn.loc.gov/2017946774

CONTENTS

CHAPTER ONE
FIRE   4

CHAPTER TWO
POLLUTION PROBLEMS   16

CHAPTER THREE
OVERFISHING LAKES   30

CHAPTER FOUR
WATER DIVERSIONS   42

CHAPTER FIVE
DAMMING THE FLOW   54

CHAPTER SIX
DEFORESTATION DAMAGE   62

CHAPTER SEVEN
A CHANGING CLIMATE   72

CHAPTER EIGHT
INVASIVE SPECIES   80

CHAPTER NINE
THE FUTURE OF LAKE
CONSERVATION   88

CAUSE AND EFFECT   98
ESSENTIAL FACTS   100
GLOSSARY   102
ADDITIONAL RESOURCES   104

SOURCE NOTES   106
INDEX   110
ABOUT THE AUTHOR   112

The 1952 fire on the Cuyahoga River was the largest in the river's history.

FIRE

Fire! Fire! Bells clanged and sirens blared as fire engines raced to the scene of a huge five-story blaze on June 22, 1969. But this was no ordinary fire. This time, a river was burning. Oily debris in northern Ohio's Cuyahoga River had been ignited by sparks from a passing train. It burned for 20 to 30 minutes and caused approximately $50,000 in damage before firefighters got it under control.[1]

This was not the first time the Cuyahoga River had caught on fire—in fact, it was the thirteenth time since 1868. Some of the previous fires were considerably larger. The 1952 fire caused more than $1.3 million in damage, and the 1912 blaze resulted in five deaths.[2]

Polluted-water signs were seen all over the country, including in California near the Mexican border in 1978, where a young boy got sick from swimming in dangerous water.

THE MAKING OF A DISASTER

It's hard to imagine a body of water catching fire. However, in the 1800s and early 1900s, most people thought nothing of dumping industrial waste and other pollutants directly into lakes and rivers, which are closely connected within freshwater ecosystems. Surely the water would dilute everything and make it harmless, they thought. "No Swimming" and "Polluted Water" signs were a common sight. In the 1960s, a northern Ohio resident described the Cuyahoga River as being as green as pea soup. In an article about the Cuyahoga, *Time* magazine wrote, "Some river! Chocolate-brown, oily, bubbling with subsurface gases, it oozes rather than flows."[3] After decades of this treatment, the river was damaged almost beyond repair.

Trash and oily waste floating on top of the polluted water created the perfect conditions for a fire.

The Cuyahoga River feeds into Lake Erie, which was in similarly bad shape. By the 1960s, it had been declared a "dead" lake. Slimy algae covered the beaches and the surface of the water. As they decayed, they sucked all the oxygen out of the water, leaving little for fish and other organisms. The lake literally stank, and heavy metal pollution made its fish unsafe for human consumption. People began calling Lake Erie "North America's Dead Sea."[4]

NOT-SO-GREAT LAKES

The Great Lakes hold more than 65 quadrillion gallons (246 quadrillion L) of water—approximately 18 percent of all freshwater on Earth's surface.[5] They are incredibly large: their combined area is approximately the size of the entire United Kingdom.[6] But despite their size, the Great Lakes have suffered serious damage as a result of human activities.

By the time the Cuyahoga River caught fire, the Great Lakes had been worsening for a long time. As the populations of major cities such as Cleveland, Ohio; Detroit, Michigan; and

RIVERS OF FIRE

In the late 1800s and early 1900s, rivers in the United States frequently caught on fire. The Cuyahoga River burned at least 13 times, and rivers in Detroit, Michigan; Baltimore, Maryland; Philadelphia, Pennsylvania; and Buffalo, New York, also caught fire. Fires on the Chicago River provided frequent entertainment to spectators. While the 1969 Cuyahoga River fire was the last river fire in the United States, other countries with more lax environmental laws still experience them. The Meiyu River in China caught fire in 2014, likely sparked by a cigarette butt. A section of Bellandur Lake in India caught fire the following year, and the fire quickly spread to nearby apartments. It is unlikely to be the last such fire, unless stronger laws are put in place around the world.

Chicago, Illinois, skyrocketed, their sewage systems did not keep pace. In the mid-1800s, many of these cities built sewage systems that emptied untreated wastewater directly into the Great Lakes. In the 1870s, for instance, Cleveland's dumping of sewage into Lake Erie made the city's water supply—which came directly from the lake—unsafe to drink. The city tried moving the sewage pipes farther out into the lake. When that did not help, it began adding chlorine to its water supply in 1911 and filtering incoming water in 1917. This cut down greatly on diseases such as typhoid and cholera, but it did not improve the health of the lake.

IS IT A LAKE OR A POND?

Lakes and ponds are both bodies of standing water. The water may come from glaciers, rivers, seepage of groundwater, or runoff from surrounding areas. So what is the difference? Surprisingly, it's not the size of the pool—it's the depth. Sunlight can reach the bottom of a pond, but not a lake. This affects the amount and type of plants that can grow in each habitat, and the animals that feed on them.

Chemical companies, paper mills, steel mills, oil refineries, and other industries also began dumping their waste into the Great Lakes and surrounding rivers during World War I (1914–1918). This waste contained high levels of phosphorus and nitrogen, which are both natural chemical elements found on Earth, along with other chemicals. Perhaps because it was the shallowest and most heavily industrialized, Lake Erie suffered the most. The excess nutrients in the wastewater caused algae to grow rapidly. As the algae died off, they used up oxygen in the lake. Much of Lake Erie's floor became a dead zone, starved of oxygen. The gooey algae made the lake water unfit for fishing, swimming, or drinking. Mats of algae washed up on the beaches, making them unappealing as well.

A TURNING POINT

By the 1960s, people were beginning to complain about Lake Erie. Activists started campaigns to save the lake, and the media increased coverage of the issue. Gradually, the situation began to get the attention of state and federal officials.

Lakes can be found on every continent on Earth—even buried under the Antarctic ice sheet. Seventy percent of lake water is found in North America, Africa, and Asia.

For many, the 1969 Cuyahoga River fire was the last straw. National outrage over this and other environmental issues prompted Congress to pass the National Environmental Policy Act (NEPA) on January 1, 1970. The Environmental Protection Agency (EPA) was founded as a result of this act. In 1972, Congress passed the Clean Water Act. It required that all US rivers be clean enough for swimming and fishing by 1983 and that discharge of pollutants be ended by 1985. In 1978, the United States and Canada signed the Great Lakes Water Quality Agreement. Its purpose was "to restore and maintain the chemical, physical, and biological integrity of the Waters of the Great Lakes."[7] Under this agreement, the two countries began working together to reduce the amount of phosphorus in the lakes and thus reduce algal blooms.

With the new legislation in place, and the public's growing awareness of pollution issues, change began to happen. The US Justice Department sued a number of major polluters of the Great Lakes and forced them to stop dumping their waste into the lakes.

The Clean Water Act's goals of making every lake fishable and swimmable have not yet been achieved, but progress has been made. The proportion of US lakes, rivers, and coastal waters deemed unsafe for swimming or fishing dropped from two-thirds in the 1970s to one-third in 2014.[8]

While several sections of the Cuyahoga River are still considered Areas of Concern, or AOC, by the EPA due to their poisoned river-bottom muds and damaged riverbanks, the river has improved significantly. It hasn't caught on fire since that fateful day in 1969, and the Northeast Ohio Regional Sewer District has spent more than $3.5 billion on cleanup and improved sewer systems. More than 60 species of fish can now be found in the Cuyahoga River.[9] Beavers burrow into its banks, and bald eagles nest nearby.

Lake Erie is no longer the scummy, smelly mess it once was, either. By the early 1990s, phosphorus

The Cuyahoga River went from a river that caught on fire to a river that people could row down.

11

MAYFLY MAYHEM

In Port Clinton, an Ohio city along the Lake Erie shore, mayflies once filled the air by the millions each spring. Attracted to city lights at night, the insects would die and accumulate in huge piles along the roadways. The large mayflies, also known by their scientific name *Hexagenia*, were annoying to humans, but they provided an essential food source for fish such as perch and walleye.

Mayfly numbers dropped sharply in the 1950s, probably as a result of phosphorus pollution. After phosphorus dumping was banned by the US and Canadian governments, the mayflies began to recover. In 1996, so many mayflies swarmed Port Clinton that they had to be removed by snowplows—37 dump truck loads full. The huge swarms even shorted out the electrical system. Annoying as the insects were, this was a good sign of the lake's return to health.

levels in Lake Erie had dropped by more than 80 percent, and the algae had decreased accordingly.[10] Its water quality had improved, and native plants had returned.

NEW CHALLENGES

Stories of lake conservation rarely have a totally happy ending, however. In the late 1980s, the invasive zebra mussel and quagga mussel found their way into Lake Erie in ballast water from ships. These shellfish cluster thickly, choking out native species and competing with them for food.

By the early 2000s, the lake faced another crisis—a huge dead zone in the center of the lake. Dead fish, birds, and salamanders started floating up on beaches as a large, toxic algal bloom appeared. These dead zones continue to form regularly as runoff of nutrients from agriculture and cities into the lake causes large amounts of algae to grow. In 2014, more than 400,000 people in the Toledo, Ohio, area were left without drinking water for days when an algal bloom moved too close to the water supply.[11] Toxins from these algae can make people sick.

Lake Erie continues to face many other challenges as well, including the growing human population near its banks. Aging sewage systems may not be able to handle the increased load. Climate change is another environmental factor that may have major effects on the lake in coming years.

ECOSYSTEMS UNDER STRESS

Most of the water we use for drinking, irrigating fields, showering, washing cars, and other everyday uses comes from freshwater ecosystems. In the United States, the average person uses approximately 100 gallons (380 L) of water per day for their basic needs. The country uses another 1,700 gallons (6,435 L) per person per day indirectly, mostly for producing food.[12] This number is double the world average.

Climate change is now causing some lakes to stratify, or separate into different temperature layers, earlier each summer. This causes the surface layer to become warmer than in years past.

Freshwater is in extremely limited supply. Less than 3 percent of the water in the world is freshwater; the rest is salt water. And only approximately 1 percent of that freshwater is surface water.[13] The rest is either locked in ice or underground. While water can be reused over and over, the supply of freshwater is threatened by pollution and other environmental threats.

Nearly 69 percent of Earth's freshwater is located in glaciers and ice caps.

Groundwater, or water from underground aquifers, is often used for drinking as well as for agriculture and industry. Groundwater is also increasingly used in the bottled water industry. In 1999, the Worldwatch Institute estimated that 42.2 trillion gallons

(159.7 trillion L) of groundwater were used each year, and that number continues to increase as Earth's population grows.[14] Because groundwater often feeds lakes and rivers, its use affects water levels in these bodies of water as well.

Scientists who study water and the water cycle are called hydrologists.

Today, one out of every three people in the world lives in a region affected by a lack of clean, safe freshwater. By 2025, two-thirds of the world's people may not have enough water for their basic needs.[15] As authors Peter Rogers and Susan Leal put it, "We have begun to find substitutes for oil; but there is no substitute for water."[16]

Humans are not the only ones threatened by environmental damage to lakes and rivers. More than 40 percent of the world's fish live in freshwater ecosystems, representing more than 10,000 species.[17] But pollution, overfishing, and other environmental threats have caused more than 20 percent of these species to become threatened, endangered, or extinct in recent decades.[18] The World Wildlife Foundation's Living Planet Report showed an 81 percent decline in populations of freshwater organisms from 1970 to 2012.[19]

While the statistics sound dire, there are signs of hope. Despite the many challenges they face, most freshwater ecosystems can recover when they are protected from further damage and restored. Innovative programs are helping do just that in many areas around the globe.

A sewage pipe in China polluted a lake in Minghu City in 2013 so badly that the entire lake was filled with dead fish.

Chapter
TWO

POLLUTION PROBLEMS

A lake's ecosystem exists in a delicate balance. Its water chemistry, physical habitat, water supply, and biological composition are complex and interconnected. When one of these factors changes, it affects all the others as well. Pollution, for example, can quickly change a lake's ecology, which is the relationships of organisms in the lake to each other and their environment.

Pollution of lakes and rivers is not a new problem. Since ancient times, people have been dumping sewage into lakes and rivers. As cities became industrialized in the 1800s, people began dumping other waste materials into lakes and rivers as well.

SOURCES OF LAKE POLLUTION

There are two different types of water pollution: point source and nonpoint source. Point source pollution happens when materials are discharged directly into the water through a ditch, pipe, container, boat, or other direct source. These include sewage that is discharged directly into lakes, waste materials pumped directly into the lake by industries, and discharges from water treatment plants. Nonpoint pollution comes from more indirect sources. It includes pesticide and fertilizer runoff from farms; oil, grease, and toxic chemicals from roads; sediment from construction sites or farmland; and acid rain.

In the 1970s and 1980s, environmental agencies focused mainly on point source pollution—that is, pollutants that are dumped directly into waterways. They made great strides in reducing this type of pollution. However, many lakes and rivers in the United States are still too polluted for swimming or fishing. Most of this pollution comes from nonpoint sources such as agricultural and urban runoff, mining, and acid rain.

AGRICULTURAL POLLUTION

Earth's growing population requires vast amounts of food. As a result, agriculture is the biggest user of water in the world, accounting for approximately two-thirds of all water usage.[1] This water comes either from underground aquifers or from surface water sources such as rivers, lakes, and reservoirs. Much of the water used to irrigate crops is lost to evaporation, and the water that does return to freshwater ecosystems often carries with it pollutants such as fertilizers and pesticides as well as sediment. Agriculture was responsible for 60 percent of the pollution found in US lakes and rivers as of the year 2000.[2]

One big problem resulting from agricultural practices is excess nitrogen and phosphorus in lakes and rivers. These nutrients come from fertilizers and manure, which are applied to fields to help plants grow better. When these nutrients run off into bodies of water, they cause too much algae to grow. When the algae die, bacteria feed on them. The bacteria use up all the available oxygen in the process, so there is little or none left for other organisms to use. These anoxic conditions kill off other life in the lake. This process is called eutrophication.

In 1971, nine people who waded into the Little Menomonee River in Wisconsin in a neighborhood cleanup effort were badly burned, and some had to be hospitalized. A plant just upstream had been dumping creosote, a chemical that comes from tar, into the stream.

Eutrophication not only causes problems for fish and other aquatic creatures, it also makes the lake less attractive for recreation. Few people want to swim or boat in a scummy, toxic lake, and fish kills make lakes less valuable for fishing as well. Property values and tourism fall as the area becomes less desirable, and the costs of treating drinking water and managing the lake increase.

Sediment deposited by soil erosion also damages lakes and rivers. Soil erosion is accelerated by farming practices such as large-scale cultivation, continuous cropping (growing the same crop on a field year after year), destruction of forests and grasslands, and overgrazing of pasture lands. When it rains, exposed soil is carried off to lakes and

When a layer of green, pungent algae covers a body of water, animals' habitats are threatened.

rivers, where it causes multiple problems. Some settles to the bottom, gradually reducing the depth of the water and smothering the organisms living there. Some stays suspended in the water, making it murky. Because it blocks light, sediment affects plant growth and, in turn, the animals that use those plants for shelter, food, and nesting sites.

THE CORE 4

Many agricultural organizations are working to promote agricultural practices that minimize damage to water resources. One such program, Purdue University's Core 4, addresses the issue of agricultural pollution in an integrated way. This program is a partnership of more than 60 farmer-led organizations, government agencies, universities, and agricultural businesses. It promotes four best management practices (BMPs). The first is conservation tillage, or leaving at least 30 percent of the soil surface covered with crop residue, such as straw or cornstalks.[3] Strips or sections of untilled land are left in the field to hold the soil in place. The second BMP is nutrient management. This is using careful planning to avoid applying excess nutrients to the field. The third is integrative pest management (IPM). This involves using the minimal amount of pesticide necessary to control pest problems and

ACID RAIN

Acid rain is one source of lake pollution. The acidity of a substance is measured with the pH scale. An acid is a substance with a pH of less than 7. Pure water has a pH of 7. Rainwater normally has a pH of approximately 5.6. However, water in the atmosphere absorbs gases, including pollutants from factories and vehicle exhaust. When these pollutants are dissolved in rainwater, they form sulfuric acid and nitric acid, lowering the pH of the water to around 4.2–4.4. This extra-acidic rain dissolves additional acid-forming compounds in soil and breaks down minerals, thereby increasing its acidity even more. It changes the pH levels of the lakes and rivers it ends up in, making them more acidic as well. Since most aquatic organisms cannot survive for long at a pH level of less than 5, severe acid rain can kill off much of the life in a lake or wetland.

using more natural methods of pest control, such as natural predators and resistant crop varieties, whenever possible. The fourth practice is the use of conservation buffers—strips of vegetation around waterways that absorb some of the runoff and nutrients before they reach the water. Together, these BMPs can reduce the amount of pollution that reaches lakes or rivers by 80 percent.[4]

MUSKEGON LAKE SUCCESS STORY

In 1985, Muskegon Lake in Michigan was declared an AOC by the EPA. Nutrient runoff caused algal blooms, and pollution from industry poisoned the lake with toxic chemicals known as polychlorinated biphenyls (PCBs), mercury, and petroleum products. Beaches were closed, and fish and other wildlife declined and became unsafe to eat.

Several restoration projects began in 2013. At the Division Street Outfall bay, 3,000 poplar saplings were planted around the lake.[5] These fast-growing trees not only absorb runoff and prevent erosion but also soak up heavy metals and other toxins and change them into nontoxic forms. When mature, the trees can be harvested for making wood products or bioenergy. Other projects included removing contaminated sediment and capping the area with clean sand to seal off any remaining pollution. Invasive plants were also removed from the shoreline and replaced with native plants.

As sediment reduces the depth of a lake, plants begin to grow on the lake bottom. This growth can choke the lake, turning it into a pond surrounded by a marsh. Ultimately, the lake may disappear altogether.

Muskegon Lake is now clean enough for people to be able to go out and sail without concern about the water quality.

Following these projects, the EPA was able to lift restrictions on using water for drinking and consuming fish and wildlife from this area.

URBAN POLLUTION

Urban pollution is another big problem affecting lakes and rivers. In fact, although they cover only 1 percent of the world's land area, urban areas pose an even greater threat to freshwater ecosystems than agriculture does.[6] Paving land and adding buildings cause long-term changes to the environment that are not easily reversed. As of 2000, nearly half of the world's population lived in cities; by 2030, this number is projected to increase to 60 percent.[7] Urban pollution comes from lawns, roads, sewage, and industry.

Freshwater mussels are often used as an indicator species for water pollution; a sort of yardstick to measure pollution. They feed by filtering water through their siphons and eating the tiny plants, animals, and other organic matter in the water. Because of this, toxic substances quickly accumulate in their bodies. When larger animals feed on the mussels, the chemicals become even more concentrated in the predators' bodies, a process known as biomagnification.

One particular threat is a group of chemicals known as organochlorines, which are often found in industrial waste. Prime examples are DDT and PCBs, both of which are now banned but are very persistent in the environment. These chemicals can interfere with the development and reproduction of wildlife. Fish affected by organochlorines may have growths, lesions, birth defects, and damaged reproductive organs and fins.

BIOMAGNIFICATION

Biomagnification is the process by which living things accumulate toxins at greater concentrations than those in which the substances occur in the environment or in food. Certain chemicals, such as chlorinated hydrocarbons, tend to be more soluble in fat than in water; that is, they do not dissolve in water but easily collect in the fatty tissues of animals. This makes these chemicals prime targets for biomagnification. They also last a long time in the environment because they are not easily broken down. As they move up the food chain, they become more and more concentrated. One of the first people to call attention to this phenomenon was Rachel Carson, who noticed that a commonly used pesticide called DDT was killing eagles, ospreys, pelicans, and other large birds. While these large birds did not consume DDT directly, they fed on fish or other animals that had eaten plants containing the pesticide. Carson's work led to the banning of DDT in the United States in the 1970s.

Another threat is mercury, a toxic chemical element found in waste from mining operations, coal-fired power plants, and trash incineration. Because of the high levels of mercury found in many fish, the EPA recommends that pregnant and nursing women eat no more than one meal of freshwater fish per week. High levels of mercury can harm a child's developing nervous system and even cause death.[8]

LAKE WASHINGTON SUCCESS STORY

Lake Washington, the second-largest lake in the state of Washington, is one of the country's most striking success stories when it comes to pollution. In the 1940s and 1950s, up to 20 million gallons (approximately 75 million L) per day of treated sewage poured directly into the lake. Levels of phosphorus rose, and the lake became murky with blue-green algae. Dead algae washed ashore and rotted. Finally, in 1963, the city of Seattle decided to take action. The sewage was rerouted to new treatment plants. There, the water was cleaned before entering the lake. With the sewage gone, the lake quickly rebounded. Its transparency increased from just 30 inches (76 cm) in 1964 to 10 feet (3 m) by 1968 and 25 feet (8 m) by 1993.[9]

Several factors contributed to the success of the Lake Washington cleanup. First, the lake is relatively deep and has a high flushing rate because a lot of water flows into and out of it. It also had a relatively short pollution history, so less pollution was concentrated in the sediment than in many other lakes.

Lake Washington's deepest point is 220 feet (67 m) below the surface.

STRYKER BAY SUCCESS STORY

Stryker Bay in Duluth, Minnesota, turned into a toxic soup as industrial pollutants were dumped in it for more than 150 years. Tar and coke factories, meatpacking plants, and other industries spewed waste into the 41-acre (16.6 ha) bay, which is located at the point where the Saint Louis River meets Lake Superior. The chemicals settled into the sediment.

In 1979, the Minnesota Pollution Control Agency (MPCA) began cleaning up the lake, and in 1983, the bay was added to the federal Superfund list. From 2006 to 2010, toxic sediments were dredged up and removed. A layer of clean sand and a specially designed carbon mat were added over the remaining sediments to keep the pollution from escaping. Native vegetation was also planted.

Today the bay is clean enough to swim in. Fish and wildlife have returned, and at least for now, the toxins appear to be contained. The EPA continues to work with US Steel in Duluth and MPCA at preventing additional contamination and addressing other contaminated areas.

WHAT IS A SUPERFUND SITE?

Superfund sites are places in the United States that have been contaminated by hazardous waste and threaten human health or the environment. As part of its Superfund program, the EPA selects these sites and places them on the National Priorities List (NPL). The agency then works with communities, industries, governments, scientists, and other groups to create a plan and clean up each site.

WHAT IS A WATERSHED?

A watershed is a section of land that all drains into the same place. Watersheds are made up of both the water that falls on the ground and the water under the ground. You can find the edges of a watershed by looking at a topographic map—one that shows the height of the land. Follow the ridges and high points that drain in the same direction. A watershed can be very small or very large. It may drain into a lake, river, bay, or wetland.

Whatever pollutants are applied within a watershed will drain into its waterways. This means that pollutants dumped directly into a lake or river are not the only ones that affect the water—chemicals applied to fields, forests, or lawns in the surrounding watershed will eventually end up there as well.

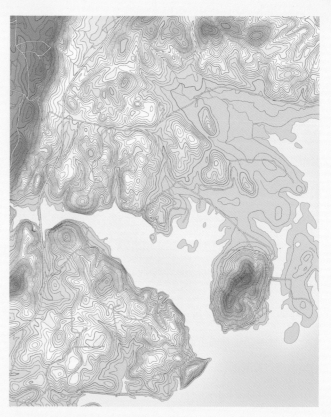

Topographical maps display levels of elevation.

The Mississippi River is part of many different watersheds.

Malawians trade fish in the village of Cape Maclear.

Chapter
THREE

OVERFISHING LAKES

Many people around the world rely on freshwater ecosystems for food. For example, in the southeastern African nation of Malawi, fish make up 70 to 75 percent of total animal protein for low-income families. Freshwater fish from the Tonlé Sap Lake in Cambodia supply approximately 60 percent of total animal protein to the population of that country.[1]

The Tonlé Sap Lake has been called Cambodia's "beating heart."[2] Its resources support more than one million people, including many who live at least part

31

Merchants who live on Tonlé Sap Lake travel by boat to other villagers' homes.

of the year in floating villages. During monsoon season, the lake floods to nearly five times its normal size.[3] The river water brings nutrients, making Tonlé Sap Lake one of the world's most productive lakes, with an annual yield of approximately 300,000 tons (272,000 metric tons) of fish.[4] However, it is also one of the world's most threatened lakes. Destruction of the surrounding mangrove forests where fish spawn, climate change, construction of hydroelectric dams, and overfishing all threaten the future of the lake, and by extension, the people around it.

When so many animals are harvested that a population cannot sustain itself, a species is said to be overexploited. Overexploitation may occur because of increasing human populations or because of improved technology. Often the animals are hunted for food. They may also be taken for the pet trade or for sport. Sometimes people hunt a species to extinction, as with the passenger pigeon in the early 1900s.

Today's fishing boats and gear are much more efficient than those of the past, leading to much larger catches of fish. In fact, the global fish harvest has

GIANTS OF THE MEKONG

In the Mekong River system of Southeast Asia, a once-important commercial fish, the Mekong giant catfish, is now nearly extinct. This large fish can grow to 10 feet (3 m) in length and weigh up to 650 pounds (300 kg), making it popular with fishers. But catfish numbers have now declined by approximately 95 percent due to overfishing, damming of rivers, and loss of habitat.[5] Perilously few are left in the wild.

quadrupled since 1950.[6] Some fishing methods have been banned in certain areas because they are too efficient. One such method is the use of gillnets, vertical sheets of netting that capture almost everything that swims through them. Another is the use of beach seines, large floating nets that are tossed out from shore.

When fish are removed from a lake faster than they can replace themselves, fewer and fewer survive to adulthood. Gradually, the average size of the fish decreases. Fishers are forced to harvest smaller and smaller fish, until eventually the animals are not old enough to reproduce before they are caught. As fewer eggs are laid, the population declines even faster.

Fish have been overharvested in many lakes; particularly in Central and South America, Africa, and Asia. In some places, this has contributed to extinction of these fish and other animals that rely on them for food. Overharvesting of lake trout in the Great Lakes and salmon in the Pacific Northwest has led to steep declines. In Africa's Lake Victoria, which borders Tanzania, Kenya, and Uganda, the number of fishers and fishing boats has quadrupled since the 1970s.[7] Between 2008 and 2010, the number of fish caught in Lake Victoria that met the government's minimum size requirements decreased by more than half.[8]

ILLEGAL FISHING METHODS

In the Euphrates basin in Raqqa, Syria, illegal fishing methods have pushed some lakes to the brink of disaster. One of these is the use of dynamite, which stuns fish and causes them

The World Wildlife Fund for Nature (WWF) has made efforts to teach villages in African countries such as Mauritania how to fish sustainably.

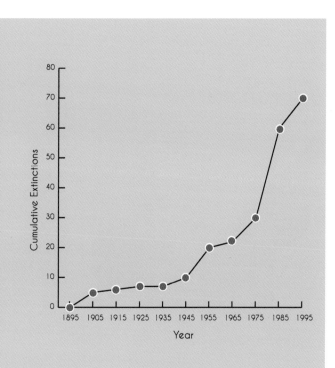

GLOBAL FISH EXTINCTIONS

It is difficult to know for sure when a fish is extinct. However, data on extinctions over the past hundred years show a growing number after World War II (1939–1945) and a steep increase after 1975. Approximately 85 percent have taken place in the past 50 years. Habitat destruction, invasive species, and overfishing are the primary causes of these extinctions.[10]

to float to the surface. It also damages the lake bottom where it is detonated and chases other fish away from the area. Generators are also used to create electric shocks that kill fish. Fishermen can catch up to 20 times as many fish using generators.[9] The shocks often kill smaller fish before they have a chance to breed. In some areas, poisons such as rotenone are even used to kill fish. These may harm people who later consume the fish.

Syria has had some success in combating these illegal fishing methods. A 2005 effort to improve Syria's Lake Dalha by more strictly enforcing laws against illegal fishing methods, educating fishers about their consequences, and stocking young fish in the lake managed to put a stop to electric shock fishing in the lake.

RETURN OF THE GAR

Prior to the 1900s, alligator gar ruled the rivers of the Midwest and Southeast United States. These giant fish could grow up to 10 feet (3 m) in length, and their

A female alligator gar can live up to 50 years in the wild.

armored scales and jagged teeth made them fearsome predators. But the gar gained a bad reputation. People called them "river pirates," arguing that they ate game fish and even humans, although there is no evidence of them doing so. Fishers hunted, shot, and dynamited alligator gar by the thousands. At the same time, the wetland

Alligator gar can weigh up to 300 pounds (140 kg).[11]

habitat they spawned in was shrinking, and dams and dikes blocked their migrations in many rivers. By the early 1900s, the alligator gar was becoming rare, and today it is at risk of extinction in some areas. In Illinois, the fish is considered extinct.

Today, scientists recognize the importance of top predators such as the alligator gar in keeping ecosystems healthy. Without them, other prized fish overpopulate and their growth is stunted because of competition for food. Some researchers are looking for ways to bring back the alligator gar. In Illinois, the fish is being restocked in Spunky Bottoms, a restored wetland belonging to the Nature Conservancy, a worldwide conservation organization. Scientists hope they may one day help control the invasive Asian carp. So far, the fish appear to be thriving. Perhaps one day the "river pirates" will again rule the rivers of Illinois and other states.

LAKE STURGEON SUCCESS

The lake sturgeon is an ancient species of fish that dates back to the era of the dinosaurs. It can grow to more than 8 feet (2.4 m) in length and weighs up to 200 pounds (90 kg).[12] The fish has a long snout and bony armor. It can be found throughout the Great Lakes Basin, and it was once abundant in the Great Lakes.

Until 1850, many fishers considered lake sturgeon a nuisance and killed them. People then began to appreciate the lake sturgeon as a food source and harvest it commercially. From 1879 to 1900, more than 4 million pounds (1.8 million kg) of sturgeon were harvested from the Great Lakes each year.[13] Along with other factors, such as damming of rivers and habitat loss, this overfishing led to a steep decline in sturgeon numbers. Today, the populations in 19 of 20 US states where the lake sturgeon lives are either threatened or endangered.[14]

There is still hope for the sturgeon, however. More than 40 groups are working together to protect and restore the fish. Some states now protect the fish during its spawning times. Others are looking at ways to allow the sturgeon to pass through dams and other blockages. Young fish known as fingerlings have been stocked in some areas to boost the population. In Canada, the lake sturgeon is protected by closed fishing seasons, size limits, and gear restrictions that make it more difficult to catch.

BELUGA STURGEON

Another type of sturgeon has not fared as well as the lake sturgeon. The beluga sturgeon lives in the Caspian Sea and is hunted for its roe, or fish eggs, which are prized as a delicacy called caviar. Females must grow for 20 years before producing roe, which they only release every three to four years. The vast majority of the world's caviar comes from beluga sturgeon, and it is in high demand. Although laws regulate the catch, fishermen still catch the fish illegally, and the population continues to decline.

The sturgeon is responding well to these protections. While its numbers are still perilously low, populations in the Great Lakes seem to be recovering slowly, over many generations. The lake sturgeon is a success story in the making, but it will require continued diligence.

WHEN THE WOLVES RETURNED

In the late 1800s and early 1900s, the wolves in Yellowstone National Park in Wyoming, Montana, and Idaho were killed off to protect livestock and wildlife that was desirable to hunters, such as deer and elk. This set off a chain of events that no one could have predicted called a trophic cascade.

With the wolves gone, the elk became more numerous. And without wolves chasing them around, they browsed more heavily than usual each winter on young trees such as willows, aspens, and cottonwoods, often in river bottoms or floodplains. This left less food for beavers, which also rely on willows for food.

It wasn't until the wolves were reintroduced to Yellowstone in 1995 that anyone realized just how profoundly they affected the ecosystem. The wolves also changed the behavior of the elk, moving them out of the valleys and gorges where they could easily be cornered. Trees in these areas grew five times taller in just six years. These new forests attracted songbirds and beavers. The beavers' dams created pools, which attracted muskrats, otters, ducks, fish, and frogs. The wolves killed coyotes, leading to an increase in mice and rabbits and their predators, such as hawks, eagles, foxes, and badgers. Bears fed on berries in the newly forested area and on carcasses the wolves left behind. They also helped control the deer.

Amazingly, even the rivers were changed by the return of the wolves. The return of these apex predators had an impact far beyond what anyone could have imagined.

Researchers at Yellowstone National Park continue to study how wolves affect the ecosystem.

The Los Angeles Aqueduct located in Owens Valley is one example of a surface water diversion.

Chapter FOUR

WATER DIVERSIONS

Surface water diversions, such as channels and pipes, are another factor affecting the flow of rivers and lakes. These diversions direct water away for irrigation, drinking water, power generation, transportation, and more. They threaten fish and other wildlife, particularly in dry climates. They also affect the communities downstream that must deal with lower water levels and decreased numbers of fish and other wildlife.

HEAT POLLUTION

One type of pollution that most people don't think about is heat pollution. Lake water is often used for cooling products or processes in power plants, steel mills, and chemical factories. The water absorbs heat, and when it is released back into the lake, it warms the area around it. Warmer water does not hold as much dissolved oxygen as cooler water can, so less oxygen is available to organisms that live there. Even a slight change in temperature can affect an animal's metabolism or a plant's growth.

IRRIGATION WATER

Irrigation of crops accounts for approximately 39 percent of freshwater use in the United States.[1] Irrigation allows farmers to grow crops in areas with dry climates or during times when rainfall is intermittent. Much of this water is used to grow grain for animal feed. It is used not only for watering plants directly, but also for applying chemicals, controlling weeds, preparing fields, harvesting, keeping down dust, and removing salts. Water is also used to irrigate golf courses, parks, plant nurseries, and cemeteries.

Unfortunately, some irrigation methods allow much of the water applied to evaporate. Irrigation water is also frequently contaminated by chemicals applied to the field and by salts that collect in the soil as the water evaporates.

Early farmers poured water onto their fields one bucketful at a time. Along the same lines, flood irrigation is still used in many parts of the world. This method consists of allowing water to flow into a field. This is the simplest and cheapest method of irrigation. However, it is wasteful, as it uses more water than necessary.

One way to lessen the demand on lakes and rivers is to use water more efficiently. Studies show that agricultural water use could be cut in half without any negative impacts

Because of its high temperatures and low precipitation, the western part of the United States uses more water for irrigation than the East.

on crops by using water-saving methods such as watering plants only when needed and transporting irrigation water in a way that prevents it from evaporating. For example, the drip irrigation method uses plastic pipes with holes in them to carry water. The pipes are laid close to a row of plants or even underground, and water drips out as it flows through the pipes. This method minimizes evaporation and uses up to 25 percent less water than flood irrigation.[2]

Spray irrigation is another common method of watering crops. In this system, tubes carry water to a series of spray guns. In very dry climates, such as the southwestern United States, however, some of the water spraying out may evaporate before it ever reaches the ground. A newer system, the Low Energy Precision Application (LEPA) center-pivot system, looks very similar. But instead of spraying the water above the crops, it gently sprays water directly down onto them. This system is 90 percent efficient and dramatically cuts down on wasted water.[3]

Technology can also help cut down on irrigation inefficiencies. Sensors can be used to measure soil water content and soil water tension. Based on these measurements, water can be applied only when needed. Measuring the water-holding capacity of the soil helps farmers know how often and how much it needs to be irrigated.

An even better solution, at least for some crops, is a technique known as dryland farming. Dryland farming dates back thousands of years in the Mediterranean region. But this ancient farming technique is finding new life in California and other western states as drought and dwindling water supplies make irrigation increasingly difficult and expensive. Dryland farmers till the soil when there is more moisture present, creating a spongy layer. The top layer is then compacted with a roller to seal in the moisture. During

Tilling is a common practice in all commercial agriculture.

BUILDING REEFS

In the Saint Clair and Detroit Rivers, artificial reefs are creating new homes for fish. Dredging rivers in the Huron-Erie Corridor made it easier for ships to pass through, but it also removed the rocky outcrops that serve as spawning grounds for many native fish species. The new reefs consist of two-foot (0.6 m) piles of rock that cover one or two acres (0.4 or 0.8 ha) of river bottom.[5] Fish such as lake sturgeon, walleye, and lake whitefish quickly began utilizing this new habitat, and the project was deemed a success.

the dry season, plants must survive on the trapped moisture and thus develop a much deeper root system than irrigated plants do. Grapes, pumpkins, apples, tomatoes, potatoes, and many other crops can be successfully dry-farmed in California. Yields may be smaller, and fruits and vegetables are generally smaller in size but sweeter and more flavorful. Few weeds can grow in the dry soil, so less weeding or herbicide use is required.

A DYING SEA

Central Asia's Aral Sea demonstrates the extreme impact water diversions can have on a body of water. Once the world's fourth-largest lake, the Aral Sea has shrunk to approximately 10 percent of its former size after decades of water diversion for irrigation and industrial water use.[4] Two major rivers that feed the lake, the Amu Darya and the Syr Darya, were diverted into the desert in the 1960s by engineers from the Soviet Union, who built dams, reservoirs, and canals to irrigate cotton and wheat fields in Kazakhstan and Uzbekistan. But the system was leaky and did not return water to the rivers, the lake's lifeblood. The lake began to shrink, becoming more and more saline as the salt grew more concentrated in a smaller amount of water. Eventually it became even saltier than the ocean. Now, nothing but a dusty, salty wasteland remains where the rest of the lake once lay.

As a result of the lake's increasing saltiness and drastically shrinking habitat, millions of fish died. The fishing industry and a muskrat pelt industry dried up. The communities that formerly lined the shores of the Aral Sea and depended on these industries for a living found themselves stranded miles from the remaining patches of water, their livelihoods gone.

Fertilizer and pesticides polluted the remaining water, and salty dust from the lake bed blew onto nearby fields. The dust contained fertilizer and pesticide residues, which can cause human health problems. Since large lakes affect local climates by absorbing heat and putting moisture into the air, the shrinking of the Aral Sea has even changed weather patterns in the region, resulting in colder winters and hotter, drier summers.

THE INS AND OUTS OF LAKE WATER

Lakes are fed by three main sources: precipitation (rain or snow), flow from streams and rivers, and groundwater. Some also receive water from melting glaciers. In a closed lake system, water cannot leave except through evaporation. In an open lake system, water can exit the lake through rivers and streams above ground or through groundwater flows underground as well as by evaporation.

In an effort to repair some of the damage, Kazakhstan built a dam between the northern and southern parts of the sea. It completely cut off the southern portion, but the water levels in the northern part have increased and become less salty. Slowly, this small portion of the lake is rebounding. It is a small success amidst a much larger tragedy.

INDUSTRY USAGE

Factories that produce food, paper, chemicals, petroleum products, and metals use large quantities of water. This water is used for making products, processing, washing, diluting, and cooling. Twenty percent of global water usage is related to industries like these, including 7 percent of water usage in the United States. Of this 7 percent, 82 percent comes from surface water. Global water use for industry is expected to quadruple by 2025.[6]

THE BOTTLED WATER BATTLE

Millions of people around the world buy bottled water because they believe it is cleaner, safer, or just more convenient than their city's tap water. But is it?

While the bottles may sport images of mountain springs, only approximately 55 percent of bottled water actually comes from natural springs. The other 45 percent is mostly municipal water—that is, tap water.[9] A high percentage of bottled water comes from places where water is scarce, such as California. In addition, manufacturing plastic bottles requires large amounts of water and petroleum, and results in additional pollution and waste. To conserve water, experts recommend buying a reusable bottle and filling it from the tap.

Studies show that by increasing efficiency, industrial water use could be cut 40 to 90 percent without any major negative impacts.[7] Many improvements have already been made. Steel factories, for instance, have reduced their water usage 10- to 16-fold in the past 70 years.[8] Water use can be reduced by educating employees about how to save water, finding leaks in the system, adding shutoff valves to hoses, adding low-flow faucets, and

Environmentalists recommend buying a reusable water bottle instead of bottled water to help the environment.

choosing water-efficient machinery. Water can also be stored and reused rather than being disposed of.

The Ford Motor Company cut its water use by 71 percent in the United States and 62 percent globally between 2000 and 2012. This resulted in a savings of 10.6 billion gallons (40.1 billion L) of water.[10] The company achieved this by using a new method of machining parts, one that used far less water and resulted in less oily wastewater to deal with. Ford also combined two steps in the painting process and set up a water treatment system that allows the company to reuse up to 65 percent of its wastewater for processes like cooling, cleaning, and irrigation.[11]

WATER USE AT HOME

Although it makes up a much smaller percentage of total water use than agriculture or industry, domestic water use also affects the supply of surface water in lakes, rivers, and reservoirs. This water is used for drinking, flushing toilets, bathing, preparing food, washing clothes, filling pools, and watering lawns and gardens.

Studies show that water usage in cities and homes could be decreased by more than 30 percent without any effect on people's lifestyles.[12] These changes may involve more efficient plumbing or fixtures as well as changes in water use that result in less waste.

Installing low-flow showerheads, low-flush toilets, and other such water-saving fixtures can save vast quantities of water. Recycling wastewater offers huge water savings as well, and many communities now use treated wastewater for factories, irrigation, and drinking.

SAVING WATER, ENERGY, AND MONEY

Canada's Cascade Tissue Group has found that going green saves money, to the tune of 24 million Canadian dollars per year. One of this company's paper factories saves 2.6 billion gallons of water (approximately 9.8 billion L) per year by using recycled fiber instead of new materials and by reusing water, either directly or after filtration. Overall, the company's water consumption is just one-fifth that of comparable companies.[13]

GROUNDWATER USAGE

Groundwater is found in aquifers, areas of permeable rock that can hold and transmit water. Aquifers fill when precipitation filters down through the soil layer to the rock below. When groundwater is used faster than it can be replaced by rainfall or snowmelt, a water deficit is created. Eventually, if the water deficit continues, the groundwater will disappear. This not only causes wells to dry up but also can affect rivers and streams that are fed by groundwater as well.

The level below which the ground is saturated with water is called the water table. If a streambed lies below the water table, water will seep from the ground into the stream. This is especially important during times of drought, when little water flows into the stream from rain runoff. The reverse is also true. Surface water from lakes, rivers, and streams seeps into the surrounding soil and helps to refill aquifers. The direction of the flow from groundwater to lakes, rivers, and streams is affected by the amount of precipitation, water levels both above and below the ground, and temperature.

An artesian well is drilled in an aquifer that has a layer of impermeable rock above and below it. Because the water is under pressure, it spurts out on its own when a well is drilled—no pump needed.

The Big Lost River in Idaho flows in the direction of river to aquifer. Water in this river flows out of a mountain valley into the Snake River Plain, where it seeps into the aquifer below and disappears. The water then flows underground to the Snake River Canyon, where it joins the Snake River via springs in the canyon walls. Groundwater sources like these are very important to maintaining the flow of the Snake River. Although diversions for irrigation cause the river to nearly dry up approximately 30 miles (50 km) south of Milner Dam in south central Idaho, springs in the Thousand Springs State Park area pump more than 37,000 gallons (140,000 L) per second back into the river.[14]

The Mansfield Dam in Austin, Texas, was created to help contain floodwaters.

Chapter
FIVE

DAMMING THE FLOW

Dams are structures built to hold back the flow of water in rivers. They can control flooding, release water for irrigation, generate hydroelectric power (electricity created when water spins turbines), and create reservoirs. But while dams provide many benefits to humans, they can harm freshwater ecosystems. These large structures block migrating fish and prevent sediments, nutrients, and water from flowing naturally through waterways.

More than 45,000 large dams disrupt rivers worldwide, affecting more than 60 percent of the world's large river basins.[1] China has more than 22,000 dams, and the United States has approximately 6,600. Another 800,000 dams worldwide block

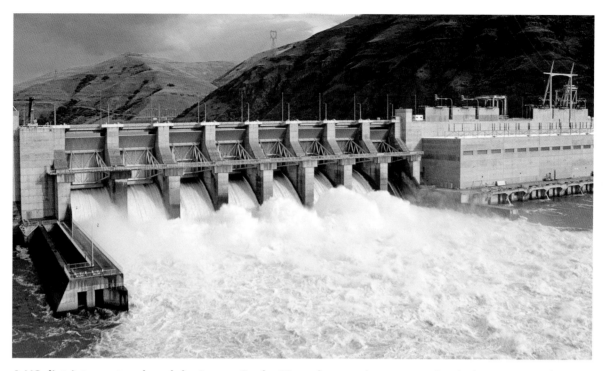

A US district court ordered the Lower Snake River dams to be removed to help protect salmon in the area.

smaller streams and rivers; 100,000 of these are in the United States.[2] These dams have had a significant impact on the flow of water through rivers, lakes, and streams. Some scientists suggest dams have even affected the speed of Earth's rotation and its tilt.

One major issue caused by dams is that they alter the natural flow pattern of rivers. Dams trap much of the coarse sediment in the water and stop it from flowing downstream. The low-sediment water that passes through tends to erode the areas below the dam. These changes in the sediment may reduce the amount of habitat available for the eggs and larvae of fish and invertebrate species. In addition, high concentrations of pollutants can build up in the sediments caught behind the dam. When water is released, these pollutants can affect areas downstream. Along with sediments, dams keep coarse woody debris (CWD) from moving downstream. CWD provides shelter and food for fish, and helps hold the sediment in place.

The higher the dam, the more energy it can produce. The amount of water flowing through the turbine also affects the amount of power produced.

Dams block fish movement as well, and dam operators must find ways to keep fish from entering turbines and pumps. Barriers such as screens can work, but they create problems when flows are too strong. Flashing lights keep fish away, but they may also cause problems by scaring away migratory fish. Acoustic transmitters show promise in this regard. They send out high-pitched noises that deter certain species of fish.

CREATIVE SOLUTIONS

While removing dams entirely may not always be practical, new management methods can help minimize their negative effects. For instance, flow releases can be timed to more closely match the natural flow of a river. When communities downstream from the Pak Mun Dam in Thailand complained of reduced fish catches, experts tried releasing higher amounts of water. After a year, not only had reservoir

HOW A LOCK WORKS

Locks allow ships to move from higher to lower water levels, or vice versa. They do this by trapping water in a chamber between two gates. When a ship approaches, it moves into the chamber. Water is added or removed to raise or lower the ship to the level of the water on the other side. Then the gates open and the ship moves on.

levels stabilized but vegetation and more than 152 species of fish had returned to the river downstream.[3]

Another major issue with dams is that they block fish such as salmon from migrating upstream to breed. Several solutions to this problem are currently in use. Fish ladders are a series of steps that fish can leap up, with a resting pool on each step. In theory, they allow fish to move between rivers and reservoirs. However, fish ladders are not terribly effective in most cases. Studies show that few fish actually make it up them; and those that do are often killed by the turbines in the dam when they try to swim back downriver. Slotted fishways are similar, but look more like slotted chutes with places for fish to rest as they move through. Another method is the lock-and-lift system, which traps fish in a chamber before moving the water level up or down. In some areas, fish are even caught and moved by tram, barge, or truck around dams. Unfortunately, many large dams, such as those on the Missouri River, lack fish ladders entirely, putting migratory fish like the pallid sturgeon in danger.

A SHAD STORY

The Alabama shad, a freshwater fish that lives in the southeastern United States, is benefiting from a new practice known as conservation locking. This practice utilizes locks that move ships past dams to move fish as well. This allows the fish to swim upstream to spawn. On the Apalachicola River in Florida, engineers added a water pump to a lock because the sound of splashing water it makes attracts fish. They then began opening and closing the lock twice per day to let fish pass through, even if there were no ships in the area. A year after this program was introduced, the shad population had increased by 122,000.[5]

DAM REMOVAL

In some places, dams have been removed to restore freshwater ecosystems. Approximately 500 US dams have been removed since 1912.[4] Most of these were

There are more than two million man-made fish barriers in the United States, including fish ladders.

small, with one of the largest being the Grangeville Dam on the Clearwater River in Idaho. This 62-foot (19 m) dam was removed to allow salmon to migrate freely upstream. Dams in France, Latvia, the Czech Republic, and Australia have also been removed to restore fish and other wildlife habitats.

The removal of the Edwards Dam on the Kennebec River in Maine is a conservation success story. Before the dam's construction in 1837, Atlantic salmon, shad, sturgeon, striped bass, and many other fish migrated through the river. The new dam provided power to local factories, but it caused a drop in the fish catch from more than 145,000 pounds (66,000 kg) per year to approximately 5,500 pounds (2,500 kg) per year by 1880.[6]

A US district judge ordered a local pharmaceutical company to clean up the mercury in the Penobscot River in 2015.

In 1989, the Kennebec Coalition began working to raise the $3 million it needed to remove the dam. The dam was removed in three stages, beginning in 1999. After its removal, fish returned to the river, followed by osprey, bald eagles, great blue herons, and other wildlife.

Another Maine river, the Penobscot, has also benefited from dam removals. A series of hydroelectric dams built approximately 100 years ago blocked the migration of Atlantic salmon, shad, sturgeon, eel, alewife, and other fish. In 2012 and 2013, thanks to a partnership between the Penobscot Nation, two hydropower companies, conservation groups, and state and federal agencies, two of the lower dams were removed. In 2016, an artificial stream was built alongside one of the remaining dams to allow the fish to bypass it.

This project gave the salmon and other fish access to 1,000 additional miles (1,600 km) of rivers and streams. The fish quickly moved in. By 2016, there were an estimated 8,000 shad in the river, and the river herring population had exploded from zero to two million.[7] These fish will provide food for other wildlife in the area, as well as for human fishers. Since many of these species migrate to the ocean, their ocean populations are expected to increase as well.

Amazingly, because of updates to the remaining dams, the power output in the area actually increased. This story is a win for the fish as well as for all those who will benefit from the increased energy production.

STREAM CROSSING

Culverts are often built to allow water to pass under a road. However, they are often too narrow, too shallow, or too high above the streambed for fish such as brook trout to migrate through. The trout normally move upstream to cooler waters in summer. When the route is blocked, they may suffer heat stress and overcrowding.

Now conservation scientists are working to identify which culverts should be modified or removed to allow the fish to pass through more easily. In the Ausable River Watershed in New York, for instance, several culverts have been replaced with bridges. Not only do the new bridges allow fish to pass through unimpeded, but they are less likely to be clogged by debris, are cheaper to maintain, and are expected to last a century.

Nearly 20 percent of the Amazon Rain Forest has been a victim of deforestation.

Chapter

SIX

DEFORESTATION DAMAGE

Deforestation—the cutting of trees for logging or agriculture—is another human activity that endangers lakes, rivers, and streams. Globally, approximately 32 million acres (13 million ha) of forest are cut down each year.[1] The drinking water for many cities is affected by this process, as are many lake and river ecosystems.

The land surrounding lakes has a surprisingly large impact on water quality. Forests, wetlands, grasslands, and floodplains surrounding lakes and rivers soak up rainwater, thus preventing flooding. Called riparian zones, they act as natural filters, collecting sediment and other pollution before it reaches the water.

WHAT IS A TREE WORTH?

Trees provide many useful products, such as logs, paper, fruit, nuts, rubber, and medicines. They offer beauty and shade from the sun. But the value of trees goes far beyond their usefulness to humans. Tree roots also hold soil in place, keeping it stable. When trees are removed from a hillside, rockslides and mudslides may occur. On flatter ground, exposed soil may wash away in the rain or simply dry up and blow away as dust, taking valuable nutrients with it.

Trees also regulate the temperature of the planet by providing shade and absorbing sunlight. As trees perform photosynthesis, they take water from the ground and return it to the atmosphere. An Earth without trees would be a much hotter, drier place. Trees also absorb carbon dioxide, a greenhouse gas, and turn it into the oxygen that humans and animals need to breathe.

Forests help hold the banks of rivers and lakes in place. When forests are cleared for construction or agriculture, rivers and lakes are more prone to flooding. Their water becomes murkier and more polluted, and ultimately less productive.

Sedimentation can affect spawning in some fish species. It makes it harder for the fish to find each other to mate, and silty riverbeds may not be suitable for laying eggs. It also makes it harder for some fish, such as young salmon, to find food. Silt can even clog the gills of fish, causing them to suffocate. In general, fish that feed or breed on lake or river bottoms suffer the most from sedimentation.

Scientists studying a Canadian lake affected by acid rain found that forested areas provide more food for fish as well. At Daisy Lake near Ontario, fish in areas with more forest cover were fatter than those in areas with less cover. The scientists believe this is because of the plant debris that falls into the water in forested areas. Bacteria feed on the debris, and are in turn eaten by tiny animals called zooplankton. Young fish then feed on the zooplankton. Many species, such as catfish, also use forest debris as spawning or resting sites.

Trees located on Mount Mitchell in North Carolina were destroyed by acid rain.

Name	Continent	Area (sq mi)	Area (sq km)
1. Lake Superior	North America	31,820	82,413
2. Lake Victoria	Africa	26,828	69,484
3. Lake Huron	North America	23,010	59,596
4. Lake Michigan	North America	22,400	58,016
5. Aral Sea	Asia	13,000	33,670
6. Lake Tanganyika	Africa	12,700	32,893
7. Lake Baikal	Asia	12,162	31,499
8. Great Bear Lake	North America	12,000	31,080
9. Lake Nyasa	Africa	11,600	30,044
10. Great Slave Lake	North America	11,031	28,570

The world's top 10 largest freshwater lakes

WATER CHANGES

Deforestation changes the chemical composition of lakes, rivers, and streams by releasing soluble minerals and nutrients from the soil. When it rains, these chemicals are carried into lakes and rivers. Bodies of water in deforested areas have higher levels of nitrates than those in forested areas. Like phosphates, nitrates can cause overgrowth of algae and other plants, leading to eutrophication.

Other substances may be released as well. For example, in the Amazon River Basin, some deforested soils release mercury into the water. This toxic element becomes more concentrated as it moves up the food chain, endangering the health of people that eat fish caught in these areas.

Water temperatures also rise slightly when forests are removed, since overhanging trees no longer shade the water. These temperature changes can affect the growth and reproduction of fish and other aquatic organisms.

CHANGING THE CLIMATE

Extensive deforestation can even change the climate. A 2010 study found that deforestation was responsible for 17 percent of all greenhouse gas emissions; that is, emissions of gases such as carbon dioxide and

Forests are being cut down at an alarming rate. An area the size of 48 football fields—more than 29 million acres (11.7 million ha)—is destroyed every minute.[2]

Technically, the world's largest lake is the Caspian Sea. The Romans called it a sea because it is salty, but geographers consider it a lake because it is completely surrounded by land.

The Amazon River Basin covers nearly 40 percent of South America.

methane that are responsible for global climate change.[3] Burning trees puts carbon into the atmosphere and decreases the number of trees available to remove carbon dioxide by photosynthesis. In addition, exposed soil receives more sunlight, which warms the soil. This warming speeds up the work of the microbes that convert carbon in the soil into carbon dioxide. Some of this carbon dioxide is then released into the atmosphere.

Tropical forests are home to more than one-half of all plants and land animals in the world. But approximately one-half of these forests have been cut down, threatening the survival of many species.[5]

In the Amazon River Basin, deforestation has made the climate drier, hotter, and less predictable. This affects the amount of rain falling on the area and thus the amount of water in the watershed. Because of deforestation, the rainy season in the Amazon is being delayed by an additional six days every ten years.[4]

Deforestation and climate change thus work together in a vicious cycle. As global climate change causes longer periods of drought, more trees die, making forests more susceptible to wildfires. These dying trees, in turn, reduce the amount of water returned to the atmosphere, thereby worsening the drought.

REVERSING THE TREND

The Nature Conservancy is one of the organizations working to counter deforestation and habitat degradation. Its Water Funds program allows people in cities to invest in the protection of upstream areas in order to protect their own water supply. In Latin America, for example, heavy water users such as municipal water suppliers, sugarcane growers' associations, breweries, and others can donate to a water fund. This money is used to replant forests and help rural people plant organic gardens or start small businesses that do not deplete water supplies. In some areas, the fund pays farmers to protect or restore riverside forests. These projects are based on the idea that it is cheaper to stop problems at the source than it is to fix them later. It is an investment in the future that is already paying off.

SLASH AND BURN

Tropical rain forests are often cleared by a method known as slash and burn. This method is exactly what it sounds like: trees are chopped down and the remaining vegetation is burned. It is usually done to convert forested areas to agricultural land, often illegally. Unfortunately, rain forest soil is not very fertile. The ash from the burned trees provides some nutrients, but these soon diminish. Within a few years, the cleared area is usually abandoned or converted to cattle pasture. The farmers must move on to another area.

Another side effect of slash and burn is that fires often spread beyond their intended boundaries, burning understory trees and brush in the surrounding forest. The dead trees left behind make the forest more prone to larger fires in the future.

THE WATER CYCLE

Most of the world's water is in continuous motion in a pattern called the water cycle or hydrologic cycle. Water in the air condenses into clouds and falls to the ground as rain or snow. Some of this water soaks into the ground and becomes groundwater. Some runs off into lakes, rivers, and streams. Some is absorbed by plants.

The water in rivers flows toward the oceans. Heat from the sun makes water from the ocean—as well as from lakes, rivers, and soil—evaporate into the air. Water that is taken up by plants is also released into the air as they breathe. As all this wet air rises, it cools and condenses into clouds, resulting in precipitation. Then the cycle begins again.

Condensation

Evaporation

Precipitation

Water can travel thousands of miles in one cycle.

Earth's lakes are getting warmer every year.

Chapter SEVEN

A CHANGING CLIMATE

Climate change is a term used to describe changes in Earth's climate caused by increased amounts of certain greenhouse gases in the atmosphere. Many of these gases are produced when fossil fuels such as coal, oil, and natural gas are burned. They trap heat in the atmosphere, causing a gradual increase in Earth's average temperature.

This increase in temperature is changing weather patterns worldwide. For instance, California, which produces much of the food consumed in the United States, is experiencing a long-term drought that has led to pitched battles over water rights. Many parts of the state are naturally dry, and climate change has made them even drier. California's population was 39.4 million in 2016, and it will likely increase to 50 million by 2055.[1] The state's growing population and agricultural production require more water each year.

The majority of climate change has taken place in the past 35 years. The years 2001 to 2017 comprised 16 of the 17 warmest years ever recorded.[6]

Climate scientists suggest that mean global temperatures may increase by as much as 2.7 to 10.4 degrees Fahrenheit (1.5 to 5.8°C) by the end of this century.[2] Warmer winter temperatures will lead to less snow cover and earlier snowmelt, change patterns of flooding and drought, and impact lakes and rivers. Higher temperatures will likely cause water to evaporate faster and reduce rainfall as well. By 2050, one billion city dwellers, especially those in countries with few resources, may need to survive on 26.4 gallons (100 L) of water per person per day—less than two-thirds of a bathtubful.[3]

A long-term study by the National Aeronautics and Space Administration (NASA) concluded that climate change is warming lakes by an average of 0.61 degrees Fahrenheit (0.34°C) per decade because of the heat-retaining properties and smaller volumes of lakes.[4] This is faster than either the atmosphere or the ocean are warming. The highest rates were found at high latitudes, where lakes are warming an average of 1.3 degrees Fahrenheit (0.72°C) per decade.[5] The ice cover of northern lakes is melting earlier in the season as well.

These numbers may sound small, but even small changes in water temperature can affect the survival and reproduction of aquatic organisms. Algal blooms are expected to increase by 20 percent over the next century, leading to a 4 percent increase in emissions of methane, a gas that has even stronger effects on the climate than carbon dioxide.[7] Warmer temperatures favor smaller fish with faster reproductive cycles, which is already leading to shifts in the dominant species in some lakes.

These changes in water temperature can also result in additional changes to the local climate. For example, the amount of ice cover on a lake affects the amount of heat and moisture that is given off or absorbed. Ice and snow reflect heat, while exposed water and soil absorb it. Snow and ice also affect how much sunlight penetrates the water, thus affecting the growth of aquatic plants and animals.

GREENHOUSE GASES

Certain types of gases can trap heat in Earth's atmosphere. These are known as greenhouse gases. Common greenhouse gases include carbon dioxide, methane, nitrous oxide, and fluorinated gases. Carbon dioxide is the most abundant. It is produced when coal, oil, wood, and other carbon products are burned. Livestock, decaying waste, and production and transport of fossil fuels put methane into the atmosphere. Nitrous oxide comes from agricultural activities and the burning of fossil fuels. Fluorinated gases are usually produced by industry.

A CHANGING LAKE

Lake Tanganyika in East Africa contains 18 percent of the world's liquid freshwater. Approximately 200,000 short tons (181,000 metric tons) of fish are harvested from this huge lake each year, supplying up to 40 percent of the animal protein consumed by people in the area.[8] However, the number of fish in Lake Tanganyika is declining.

A 2016 study of Lake Tanganyika showed a clear effect of climate change on the productivity of the lake. The researchers studied fossils in the lake's sediments to trace the numbers of fish over the past 1,500 years. Their studies showed that as water temperature began to rise in the 1800s, numbers of fish began to decline.

As the lake warms, the lake floor is losing oxygen, killing animals such as freshwater snails that live there. The warmer temperatures also prevent the mixing of the three major layers that make up lakes. Reduced mixing of the layers means that fewer nutrients make it to the top of the lake, affecting the survival of algae and herbivorous fish in this layer. Less oxygen reaches the lake bottom, reducing the number of mollusks and arthropods there. Scientists say that any plans for improving the health of Lake Tanganyika must take this factor into account. They suggest that the same process is occurring in other lakes as well.

THE LAYERS OF A LAKE

Most lakes can be divided into three major zones: the littoral zone, the limnetic zone, and the profundal zone. The littoral zone consists of shallow areas where light reaches the bottom of the lake and allows rooted plants to grow. Some light also penetrates the limnetic zone. Tiny plants and animals called plankton can live there. No light reaches the profundal zone in the depths of the lake. Only a few specially adapted organisms can survive there.

THE DISAPPEARING LAKE

Lake Chad was once the sixth-largest lake in the world and the second-largest in Africa. Since the 1960s, however, Lake Chad has shrunk by 90 percent, mainly due to climate change and the overuse of water resources.[9] The changing climate is causing longer periods of drought and decreasing the amount of rainfall in the area. The shrinking lake threatens the health and livelihoods of the 30 million people that live in the lake basin.

In 2014, five countries in the Lake Chad Basin received a $78.8 million loan from the African Development Bank to help protect water resources, develop sustainable businesses, and strengthen existing programs. The goal is to strengthen the economy and protect the lake resources in a sustainable way. Only time will tell if the damage to this crucial resource can be reversed.

Since the 1800s, average annual temperatures have increased by approximately 2 degrees Fahrenheit (1.1°C) worldwide.[11]

LAKE ELSINORE RESTORATION

At the end of the 1900s, Lake Elsinore, a large lake in Southern California, faced a variety of problems. The lake level was dropping several feet every year as water evaporated at a faster rate than it could recharge. In addition, pollutants flowing into the lake from the San Jacinto Watershed led to large algal blooms, which depleted the lake's oxygen supply. Few fish, other than carp and other tolerant species, could survive these conditions, and massive fish kills occurred. Bottom-feeding fish fed on the eggs of more desirable fish such as bass and catfish, reducing their numbers still further.

That all changed in the spring of 2000, when voters in California approved a statewide water bond that provided funding to restore the lake and watershed. Officials added pumps, aeration lines, and lake-mixing fans to stir up and add oxygen to the water. In 2003, they removed more than 7,000 pounds (3,000 kg) of carp per day. By 2008, carp made up only 43 percent of the lake's fish population, as opposed to 90 percent when the program began.[10]

Lake Elsinore is located in the city of the same name.

Three groundwater wells in the area were then restored, adding more than one billion gallons (3.8 billion L) of groundwater to the lake each year. A new treatment plant was added to clean up wastewater entering the lake, and a new pipeline now delivers more than 4.5 million gallons (17 million L) of recycled water per day into the lake.[12] The nearby Canyon Lake was dredged to keep sediment from this lake from flowing into Lake Elsinore. Finally, thousands of striped bass were added to the lake to help balance the ecosystem.

The project was a resounding success. Today, the lake is a popular destination for campers, anglers, and boaters. It is a model for the restoration of other lakes as well.

CLIMATE CHANGES THE COLORADO RIVER

The Colorado River flows from the Rocky Mountains almost 1,500 miles (2,000 km) south to the Gulf of California, providing water to 30 million people. At least 70 percent of the water is diverted along the way to irrigate 3.5 million acres (1.4 million ha) of crops.[13] By the time the river reaches its mouth in the Gulf of California, it has completely disappeared. Bad news is in store for the remaining water. Scientists predict climate change will decrease the amount of precipitation in the Rocky Mountains, extend periods of drought, and cause more rapid evaporation. These changes may decrease the flow of the Colorado by 5 to 20 percent in the next four decades.[14]

Asian carp are considered an invasive species by the EPA.
They are a huge threat to native species in the Great Lakes.

Chapter
EIGHT

INVASIVE SPECIES

Invasive species are a growing threat to many lakes and rivers. These are non-native species that are introduced to an area and cause harm to native species and/or the habitat itself. In lakes, the introduction of non-native plants, fish, and other animals can lead to the extinction or endangerment of native species.

Invasive species are often introduced by humans, either on purpose or accidentally. Some of today's problem species escaped smaller ponds where they were raised for food; others were intentionally released into lakes for sport. Still others were released by aquarium owners.

Canals are another big factor in the introduction of invasive species to freshwater lakes. For millennia, people sought ways to move goods across

Some invasive species can latch onto the bottoms of boats, so when boats are moved from one body of water to another, the species is able to spread.

continents more easily. Canals, man-made waterways that connect larger bodies of water, proved to be the solution to this problem.

But the canals brought a new set of problems. By connecting previously unconnected waterways, they allowed organisms to move between bodies of water much more easily.

Some organisms swam or floated directly through the canals; others were carried on the hulls of ships. Still others traveled in ballast—tanks of water carried by ships for balance.

Plants or animals living outside their natural range are called introduced, exotic, or non-native species. When these organisms spread uncontrollably, they are called invasive species.

MUSSEL MADNESS

The first canal to open up the Great Lakes was the Erie Canal, which was completed in 1825. This canal joined the Hudson and Niagara Rivers in New York. Other canals soon followed. Although canals became less popular once railroads came into use near the end of the 1800s, the United States and Canada continued to rework their waterways.

In 1959, the Saint Lawrence Seaway opened, making it possible for ships to travel from Duluth, Minnesota, all the way to the Atlantic Ocean. Ships entering the seaway began to dump their ballast water in the Great Lakes. This unleashed an ecological disaster in the form of zebra and quagga mussels. Native to the Black and Caspian Seas, the dime-sized mussels multiplied exponentially. Today, trillions of mussels coat the bottom of the lakes and any objects they come in contact with.[1] Not only do they outcompete native mollusks for food, they plug pipes, cover boat bottoms, and cut swimmers' feet. In 1989, mussels clogged a three-foot (0.9 m) pipe in Lake Erie, cutting off the water supply to approximately 50,000 people in the city of Monroe, Michigan, for two days.[2]

Each tiny mussel can produce an astounding one million eggs per year, and there are few native predators in North America to keep these species in check. They are filter

Zebra mussels from Lake Erie cling onto a boat propeller.

feeders, feeding on tiny plankton in the water. Lakes infested by zebra and quagga mussels have become unnaturally clear because of this filtering action. Other plankton-feeding animals cannot compete, causing native species to decline and food webs to collapse.

ASIAN CARP INVADE

In the early 2000s, escaped Asian carp from fish farms in the southern United States began making their way northward through the Mississippi River. Two of these species, the bighead and silver carp, feed on plankton, gobbling up to 20 pounds (9 kg) per day and outcompeting native species for food. Bighead carp can grow to more than 100 pounds (45 kg) in size. In some rivers in the Mississippi River Basin, Asian carp make up more than 90 percent of the biomass.[3] Silver carp are also easily startled by boat motors, and have been known to injure boaters as they jump out of the water.

BALLAST WATER SOLUTIONS

Since the Saint Lawrence Seaway opened in 1959, 54 invasive species have entered the Great Lakes in ballast water.[4] Since 1993, the law has required ships to empty their ballast tanks and refill them with ocean water before entering the Great Lakes. Many freshwater organisms cannot survive in ocean water. Unfortunately, however, some can. Environmental groups like the National Wildlife Federation believe the laws are not strict enough to prevent more invaders like the zebra mussel from finding their way into the lakes in the future.

As the carp moved closer and closer to Lake Michigan, government officials decided something had to be done. Engineers got to work building an electronic barrier in the Chicago River to stop the carp from crossing into the lake. Today, this barrier is the only thing stopping the carp from spreading into the Great Lakes, which would likely lead to

Approximately 50,000 introduced species can be found living in the United States. Of these, approximately 4,300 have become invasive.[7]

disastrous results for native fish and the ecosystem in general. And they may already be there—scientists have found traces of carp DNA upstream from the barrier.

SEA LAMPREY SOLUTIONS

The control of the invasive sea lamprey is a lake conservation success story that is still being written. Lampreys are bloodsucking fish that latch onto larger fish to feed. Their round mouths are filled with sharp teeth and a rasping tongue that can cut through scales and skin. Each lamprey can kill up to 40 pounds (18 kg) of fish over its adult lifetime, approximately 12 to 18 months.[5]

Four native lamprey species can be found in the Great Lakes Basin, but their populations have never gotten out of control. This is not the case with the sea lamprey. Sea lampreys swam through shipping canals into Lake Ontario in the 1830s. Niagara Falls prevented them from spreading to the other lakes for a time. Then the construction of the Welland Canal connecting Lake Erie and Lake Ontario gave them access to the remaining lakes. By 1938, sea lampreys had reached all of the Great Lakes.

The lampreys quickly became a huge problem. Due in part to sea lamprey predation, the lake trout harvest in Lakes Huron and Superior dropped from 15 million pounds (6.8 million kg) per year before the lamprey invasion to just 300,000 pounds (136,000 kg) per year by the 1960s.[6] Many other species of fish were affected as well.

In 1955, the United States and Canada created the Great Lakes Fisheries Commission (GLFC) with the goal of solving the sea lamprey problem and keeping the lakes productive. As a result, sea lamprey numbers have been reduced by 90 percent since the 1950s.[8] A four-pronged approach was used. First, a lampricide is routinely applied to approximately 175 streams that feed into the Great Lakes.[9] This chemical kills lamprey larvae but does not affect other fish. Second, males are captured when they migrate into streams surrounding Lakes Michigan and Huron. They are sterilized and released back into the wild. These males mate with females, who are then unable to produce young. Third, physical and electrical barriers block lampreys from migrating upstream to spawn but allow other fish to pass through. Fourth, traps throughout the Great Lakes catch lampreys on their way to spawn.

TROUT WARS

While organizations are working hard to return lake trout to Lake Superior, Yellowstone National Park officials are trying to get rid of them. The fish, which were likely introduced intentionally (and illegally) from nearby lakes, have had a negative impact on the native cutthroat trout. Many kinds of wildlife rely on cutthroat trout for food, so their absence affects the whole ecosystem. The National Park Service (NPS) is using gillnets to remove the lake trout, while encouraging anglers to catch and kill the trout. The program seems to be succeeding; the number of trout in the lake increased until 2011 but has been decreasing since that time.

Along with battling the lamprey, the GLFC began stocking fertilized lake trout eggs in certain areas. The numbers of lake trout once again began to climb. It took more than 50 years, but the number of trout in Lake Superior has returned to its pre-lamprey level. While the battle is not over, progress is being made.

The water quality of the Detroit River has improved greatly since 1972, when the Clean Water Act was signed.

THE FUTURE OF LAKE CONSERVATION

Conservation science has come a long way since the Cuyahoga River caught fire in 1969, spurred by public outrage and by the formation of the EPA and the Clean Water Act in the United States. But serious problems remain. As Earth's population grows and the supply of freshwater decreases, it is critical that we find new ways to preserve and protect freshwater ecosystems.

Some have suggested desalinating ocean water as a solution to the world's water shortage. However, this solution requires a lot of energy from fossil fuels, and thus contributes to climate change. It is also very expensive. Relying on desalinated water would make food and other products cost much more. A much better solution is to conserve the freshwater we have to ensure that everyone has enough for their needs.

IT TAKES A COMMUNITY

In some areas, organizations are finding ways to work with Native communities to protect lakes and rivers. For example, on Prince of Wales Island in southeastern Alaska, the Haida Nation is working together with the Nature Conservancy to protect salmon spawning streams. Logging around the streams in past decades damaged the streams, leading to fewer salmon and steelhead trout. The Nature Conservancy is training members of this

The Nature Conservancy has worked with communities in Maine to help protect baby oysters by bringing them to a preserve.

The average US household uses 400 gallons (1,514 L) of water every day.[1]

community to collect data on stream flow, water temperature, and habitat conditions. The data will be used to assess and hopefully protect the streams in the future.

Another successful program is protecting lakes and ponds in the Philippines. Bulusan Volcano National Park is a 9,076-acre (3,673 ha) refuge surrounded by rain forest. The park contains four craters and four hot springs as well as numerous other lakes and ponds. These provide drinking and irrigation water for the surrounding communities. However, the forest has been threatened by illegal farming. To help save the forest, a preservation program hired local people to care for and replant trees in damaged areas and trained others to guide tourists, run shops, and rent kayaks. This created a new appreciation for the forest's value as it generated income through nature-based tourism.

"Clearly, we must act now if this precious freshwater heritage is to remain. We must alter our practices so that these ecosystems continue to support both freshwater biodiversity and human life. Our survival and obligation of stewardship demands that we help these freshwater ecosystems to remain healthy, properly functioning, and capable of supporting viable populations of native plants and animals."[2]

—Nicole Silk, coeditor of A Practitioner's Guide to Freshwater Biodiversity Conservation

TAKING ACTION AT HOME

One way many people are working to make change is by getting involved with local water conservation projects. These are often listed with a state's department of natural resources or local universities. Conservation organizations like the Nature

Conservancy, the Izaak Walton League, and Ducks Unlimited also provide information and opportunities.

Another powerful way citizens can make change is by voting for stronger protections for lakes and rivers. While the Clean Water Act helped to clean up and protect many freshwater ecosystems, stronger legislation may still be needed to preserve these resources in coming years.

Even those who are not old enough to vote can still help change laws to protect lakes and rivers. Writing letters to government representatives encourages them to vote to protect waterways. Writing letters to the editor of a city or school newspaper and sharing these concerns helps others understand the importance of protecting freshwater resources.

PROTECTING ENDANGERED SPECIES

One law that has significantly affected freshwater ecosystems is the Endangered Species Act, which was passed by the US government in 1973. This act recognized that many species were threatened with

WAYS TO PROTECT OUR FRESHWATER ECOSYSTEMS

There are plenty of things people can do to contribute to saving our freshwater ecosystems. For instance, it's important to not put household chemicals, medicines, or other harmful substances into the water by flushing them, putting them down the drain, or dumping them outside. Most municipal areas have approved disposal outlets.

It is also important to not waste water. Everyone should turn off the faucet when brushing their teeth or washing their hands. Be sure to flush the toilet only when necessary.

There are also water-saving washing machines and dishwashers that can be used. Wait to wash laundry until there is a full load. If it's necessary to run a smaller load, adjust the water level on the machine so it does not fill all the way.

Another way to help Earth's freshwater ecosystems is to create a compost pile or worm bin to dispose of food scraps instead of using a garbage disposal. Not only does this save water, but the compost created is great for growing plants.

Last, everyone should purchase a reusable water bottle and fill it from the tap instead of buying bottled water.

extinction and declared that they must be protected. Federal agencies were ordered to cooperate with state agencies to conserve and protect these species. As of 2017, approximately 1,652 US species are listed as endangered or threatened.[3] Aquatic animals such as fishes, crustaceans, clams, and amphibians make up a disproportionate number of these species. Efforts to protect many of these species are ongoing.

Other organizations and governments are working to identify and protect endangered species as well. Globally, the International Union for Conservation of Nature (IUCN) maintains a list of species and their conservation statuses called the IUCN Red List. This database is available online, and users can easily search for a species's status. This information can be used to determine which species are in need of protection and how best to protect them.

The pinstripe damba, native to Madagascar, is categorized as critically endangered on the IUCN Red List.

U.S. EPA
SUPERFUND
CLEANUP SITE

Governments around the world should continue to make efforts to help keep our freshwater lakes and the environment clean.

It may seem that the problems facing our world are too complex for anyone to solve. However, as anthropologist Margaret Mead once said, "Never doubt that a small group of thoughtful, committed citizens can change the world. Indeed, it's the only thing that ever has."[4] This is as true as ever when it comes to conserving lakes, rivers, and streams. Prevention is the best cure, but it's never too late to make changes to protect the freshwater ecosystems we rely on for food and water—which is to say, for life itself.

NATURESERVE

It is important to understand an ecosystem in order to know how best to protect it. One nonprofit organization that is working toward that goal is the NatureServe Network (natureserve.org). NatureServe works with 80 partners in the United States, Canada, Latin America, and the Caribbean to collect data about species and ecosystems. It makes that information available in easily understandable forms, such as maps, videos, and infographics. This allows people to make informed choices about how to best protect biodiversity in these areas. In Delaware and Maryland, for example, NatureServe Network programs created a plan to save the rare black-banded sunfish based on the data they collected. These attractive little fish are threatened by habitat loss, invasive species, and the illegal aquarium pet trade.

CAUSE AND
EFFECT

Overfishing

Stricter laws

Deforestation

Tree replanting

Pollution

Climate
change

Water diversion

Dams

Invasive species

PROTECTING FRESHWATER LAKES

Dry farming methods
Increased efficiency

Removal of dams
Restoration of streams and rivers to natural conditions

Reduction of pesticide use
Prevention of invasions

99

ESSENTIAL
FACTS

WHAT IS HAPPENING

Lakes, rivers, and streams around the world face many different threats. Scientists are working to find new ways to protect and preserve these valuable resources.

THE CAUSES

Key threats to freshwater ecosystems include pollution, deforestation, dams, diversions, invasive species, climate change, and overfishing. In many cases, these waters face multiple threats.

KEY PLAYERS

The key players in this situation are farmers, industries, fishermen, and all who rely on the health of lakes and rivers in their watershed for drinking water, food, recreation, and other resources.

WHAT IS BEING DONE TO FIX THE DAMAGE

The US Environmental Protection Agency currently monitors the health of US lakes and rivers. In some instances, it requires polluters to clean up their acts. State and local governments and environmental agencies are also working to clean up polluted or deforested lake and river ecosystems.

WHAT IT MEANS FOR THE FUTURE

Freshwater ecosystems continue to face serious challenges for the future. These include climate change, deforestation, overfishing, pollution, and more. As the human population continues to grow, these problems will multiply unless strong steps are taken to combat them.

QUOTE

"Clearly, we must act now if this precious freshwater heritage is to remain. We must alter our practices so that these ecosystems continue to support both freshwater biodiversity and human life. Our survival and obligation of stewardship demands that we help these freshwater ecosystems to remain healthy, properly functioning, and capable of supporting viable populations of native plants and animals."

—*Nicole Silk, coeditor of* A Practitioner's Guide to Freshwater Biodiversity Conservation

GLOSSARY

ALGAE

Plantlike organisms that have no true roots, stems, or leaves.

ANOXIC

Having little or no oxygen present.

BALLAST

Water, rocks, sand, or other heavy material carried aboard a ship to help stabilize it.

BIOENERGY

Energy produced from biofuels such as wood or ethanol.

BIOMAGNIFICATION

The process by which a compound, such as a pollutant or pesticide, increases its concentration in the tissues of organisms as it travels through the food web.

BIOMASS

An amount of living things in an area.

DEBRIS

The remains of something that has been broken down or destroyed.

DESALINATED

To have removed the salt from water.

ECOSYSTEMS

Communities of interacting organisms and their environment.

EROSION

The process by which Earth's surface is worn away by water, glaciers, wind, etc.

EUTROPHICATION

An accumulation of nutrients in a lake that results in the overgrowth of algae; the algae use up oxygen as they decay.

EXTINCTION

The point where individuals of a species no longer remain.

HABITAT

The natural environment of an organism.

IRRIGATION

The application of water to agricultural fields to help plants grow.

METABOLISM

The chemical reactions that occur in a living organism, such as digestion and movement of chemicals to different cells.

OVEREXPLOITATION

Use of a resource to the point that it cannot be sustained or replaced.

PHOTOSYNTHESIS

The process used by plants and other organisms to convert sunlight into usable energy.

RESERVOIRS

Places where water is stored for later use.

RIPARIAN

Related to the bank of a river or other body of water.

SALINE

Salty or saltlike.

SEDIMENTATION

The accumulation of minerals or organic matter in an area.

SPAWN

To produce eggs in a large quantity.

TURBINES

Machines with spinning blades powered by fluid or air passing through them.

ADDITIONAL RESOURCES

SELECTED BIBLIOGRAPHY

Cooke, G. Dennis. *Restoration and Management of Lakes and Reservoirs*. 3rd ed. Boca Raton, FL: Taylor & Francis/CRC, 2005. Print.

"Cuyahoga River Fire." *Ohio History Central*. Ohio History Connection, n.d. Web. 28 Mar. 2017.

Dempsey, Dave. *On the Brink: The Great Lakes in the 21st Century*. East Lansing, MI: Michigan State UP, 2004. Print.

Rogers, Peter, and Susan Leal. *Running out of Water: The Looming Crisis and Solutions to Conserve Our Most Precious Resource*. New York: St. Martin's Press, 2010. Print.

FURTHER READINGS

Barker, Geoff. *World at Risk: Water*. W. B. Saunders, 2011. Print.

Haugen, David. *Will the World Run Out of Fresh Water?* Greenhaven, 2012. Print.

Kaye, Cathryn Berger and Philippe Cousteau. *Going Blue: A Teen Guide to Saving Our Oceans, Lakes, Rivers, & Wetlands*. Minneapolis, MN: Free Spirit, 2010. Print.

Nichols, Susan. *The Politics of Water Scarcity*. Greenhaven, 2017. Print.

ONLINE RESOURCES

Booklinks
NONFICTION NETWORK
FREE! ONLINE NONFICTION RESOURCES

To learn more about freshwater lakes conservation, visit **abdobooklinks.com**. These links are routinely monitored and updated to provide the most current information available.

MORE INFORMATION

For more information on this subject, contact or visit the following organizations:

The Nature Conservancy
4245 N. Fairfax Drive, Suite 100
Arlington, VA 22203-1606
703-841-5300
nature.org

The Nature Conservancy's mission is to protect nature for people today and for future generations.

United States Environmental Protection Agency (EPA)
Environmental Protection Agency
1200 Pennsylvania Avenue, NW
Washington, DC 20460
epa.gov

The EPA's mission is to protect human health and the environment.

SOURCE NOTES

CHAPTER 1. FIRE

1. "Cuyahoga River Fire." *Ohio History Connection*. Ohio History Connection, n.d. Web. 19 Sept. 2017.

2. Ibid.

3. Dave Dempsey. *On the Brink: The Great Lakes in the 21st Century*. Lansing, MI: Michigan State UP, 2004. Print. 119.

4. Dan Egan. *The Death and Life of the Great Lakes*. New York: W. W. Norton & Company, 2017. Print. 219.

5. Dave Dempsey. *On the Brink: The Great Lakes in the 21st Century*. Lansing, MI: Michigan State UP, 2004. Print. 241.

6. "Physical Features of the Great Lakes." *EPA*. United States Environmental Protection Agency, 21 Sept. 2016. Web. 19 Sept. 2017.

7. "About the Great Lakes Water Quality Agreement." *Binational*. Canada-United States Collaboration for Great Lakes Water Equality, n.d. Web. 19 Sept. 2017.

8. Dan Egan. *The Death and Life of the Great Lakes*. New York: W. W. Norton & Company, 2017. Print. 117.

9. Christopher Maag. "From the Ashes of '69, A River Reborn." *New York Times*. New York Times, 20 June 2009. Web. 19 Sept. 2017.

10. Dave Dempsey. *On the Brink: The Great Lakes in the 21st Century*. Lansing, MI: Michigan State UP, 2004. Print. 216.

11. John Seewer. "EPA Won't Declare Lake Erie's Waters in Ohio Impaired." *U.S. News*. U.S. News & World Report, 23 May 2017. Web. 19 Sept. 2017.

12. Peter Rogers and Susan Leal. *Running out of Water: The Looming Crisis and Solutions to Conserve Our Most Precious Resource*. New York: St. Martin's Press, 2010. Print. 3.

13. "The World's Water." *USGS*. The USGS Water Science School, 2 Dec. 2016. Web. 19 Sept. 2017.

14. Dave Dempsey. *On the Brink: The Great Lakes in the 21st Century*. Lansing, MI: Michigan State UP, 2004. Print. 234.

15. "Threats to Rivers, Lakes and Wetlands." *WWF*. World Wide Fund for Nature, n.d. Web. 19 Sept. 2017.

16. Peter Rogers and Susan Leal. *Running out of Water: The Looming Crisis and Solutions to Conserve Our Most Precious Resource*. New York: St. Martin's Press, 2010. Print. 2.

17. Nicole Silk and Kristine Ciruna. *A Practitioner's Guide to Freshwater Biodiversity Conservation*. Washington, DC: Island Press, 2005. Print. 29.

18. "Freshwater Threats." *National Geographic*. National Geographic Society, n.d. Web. 19 Sept. 2017.

19. "Living Planet Index." *WWF*. World Wide Fund for Nature, n.d. Web. 19 Sept. 2017.

CHAPTER 2. POLLUTION PROBLEMS

1. Nicole Silk and Kristine Ciruna. *A Practitioner's Guide to Freshwater Biodiversity Conservation*. Washington, DC: Island Press, 2005. Print. 145.

2. Ibid. 146.

3. Ibid. 151-152.

4. Ibid. 161.

5. "Muskegon Lake's Contaminated Sediment Cleaned Up by Poplar Trees." *Healthy Lakes*. Great Lakes Coalition, 27 Aug. 2014. Web. 9 May 2017.

6. Nicole Silk and Kristine Ciruna. *A Practitioner's Guide to Freshwater Biodiversity Conservation*. Washington, DC: Island Press, 2005. Print. 172.

7. Ibid. 171.

8. Stephan Bose-O'Reilly, Kathleen M. McCarty, Nadine Steckling, and Beate Lettmeier. "Mercury Exposure and Children's Health." *NBCI*. US National Library of Medicine, Web. 19 Sept. 2017.

9. "The Lake Washington Story." *King County*. King County, n.d. Web. 19 Sept. 2017.

CHAPTER 3. OVERFISHING LAKES

1. Nicole Silk and Kristine Ciruna. *A Practitioner's Guide to Freshwater Biodiversity Conservation*. Washington, DC: Island Press, 2005. Print. 228.

2. Chris Berdik. "Of Fish, Monsoons and the Future." *New York Times*. New York Times, 9 June 2014. Web. 19 Sept. 2017.

3. Ibid.

4. Ibid.

5. "Mekong Giant Fish." *National Geographic*. National Geographic Society, n.d. Web. 19 Sept. 2017.

6. James Owen. "Overfishing Is Emptying World's Rivers, Lakes, Experts Warn." *National Geographic*. National Geographic Society, 1 Dec. 2005. Web. 11 May 2017.

7. Rowena Ryan. "Africa's Biggest Lake Is on the Verge of Dying." *News.com.au*. News Limited, 2 Apr. 2015. Web. 19 Sept. 2017.

8. Tim McDonnell. "One of the World's Biggest Lakes Is Dying and We're To Blame." *Mother Jones*. Mother Jones, 30 Jan. 2015. Web. 19 Sept. 2017.

9. "Overfishing Exhausts Fish Resources in the Euphrates and Threatens Consumers' Health." *Arab Reporters for Investigative Journalism*. Arab Reporters for Investigative Journalism, 17 Dec. 2009. Web. 16 Apr. 2017

10. Gene S. Helfman. *Fish Conservation: A Guide to Understanding and Restoring Global Aquatic Biodiversity and Fishery Resources*. Washington, DC: Island Press, 2007. Print. 7–8.

11. "Alligator Gar." *National Geographic*. National Geographic Society, n.d. Web. 19 Sept. 2017.

12. "Lake Sturgeon Fact Sheet." *Great Lakes Inform*. Great Lakes Inform, n.d. Web. 19 Sept. 2017.

13. Ibid.

14. Ibid.

CHAPTER 4. WATER DIVERSIONS

1. "Irrigation Techniques." *USGS*. The USGS Water Science School, 2 Dec. 2016. Web. 19 Sept. 2017.

2. Ibid.

3. "Irrigation Water Use: Low-Energy Spray Irrigation." *USGS*. The USGS Water Science School, 2 Dec. 2016. Web. 19 Sept. 2017.

4. Dan Egan. *The Death and Life of the Great Lakes*. New York: W. W. Norton & Company, 2017. Print. 266.

5. "Artificial Reefs a Success in the Huron-Erie Corridor." *Fish and Wildlife Service*. US Fish and Wildlife Service, 2 July 2013. Web. 19 Sept. 2017.

6. Nicole Silk and Kristine Ciruna. *A Practitioner's Guide to Freshwater Biodiversity Conservation*. Washington, DC: Island Press, 2005. Print. 173.

7. Nicole Silk and Kristine Ciruna. *A Practitioner's Guide to Freshwater Biodiversity Conservation*. Washington, DC: Island Press, 2005. Print. 102.

8. Ibid. 103.

SOURCE
NOTES *CONTINUED*

9. Julia Lurie. "Bottled Water Comes from the Most Drought-Ridden Places in the Country." *Mother Jones.* Mother Jones, 11 Aug. 2014. Web. 28 Apr. 2017.

10. Jaan Koel. "How 5 Manufacturers Reduce Water Use." *Fabricators & Manufacturers Association International.* Fabricators & Manufacturers Association International, 27 July 2013. Web. 30 Apr. 2017.

11. Ibid.

12. Nicole Silk and Kristine Ciruna. *A Practitioner's Guide to Freshwater Biodiversity Conservation.* Washington, DC: Island Press, 2005. Print. 102.

13. Jaan Koel. "How 5 Manufacturers Reduce Water Use." *Fabricators & Manufacturers Association International.* Fabricators & Manufacturers Association International, 27 July 2013. Web. 30 Apr. 2017.

14. Dr. Gary Johnson, Donna Cosgrove, and Mark Lovell. "What Is Meant by 'Surface and Ground Water Interaction?'" *Idaho Water Resource Research Institute.* University of Idaho. Dec. 1998. Web. 19 Sept. 2017.

CHAPTER 5. DAMMING THE FLOW

1. Nicole Silk and Kristine Ciruna. *A Practitioner's Guide to Freshwater Biodiversity Conservation.* Washington, DC: Island Press, 2005. Print. 68-69.

2. Ibid. 68.

3. Ibid. 72.

4. Ibid. 80.

5. Matt Miller. "Results: Great News for Shad." *Nature.org.* The Nature Conservancy, 18 Apr. 2013. Web. 19 Sept. 2017.

6. Nicole Silk and Kristine Ciruna. *A Practitioner's Guide to Freshwater Biodiversity Conservation.* Washington, DC: Island Press, 2005. Print. 82.

7. "Fact Sheet 2016." *Penobscot River.* Penobscot River Restoration Trust, n.d. Web. 19 Sept. 2017.

CHAPTER 6. DEFORESTATION DAMAGE

1. "Why Is Our Water in Trouble?" *Nature.org.* The Nature Conservancy, n.d. Web. 19 Sept. 2017.

2. "Deforestation." *WWF.* World Wide Fund for Nature, n.d. Web. 19 Sept. 2017.

3. Scott Auerbach. "Deforestation Effects on Ecosystems." *Sciencing.* Leaf Group Ltd., 24 Apr. 2017. Web. 19 Sept. 2017.

4. Lynn Davis. "Climate Change, Dams, Deforestation a Vicious Cycle for Amazon Rivers, Lakes." *Phys.org.* Science X Network, 1 Mar. 2016. Web. 17 Apr. 2017.

5. Alina Bradford. "Deforestation: Facts, Causes & Effects." *LiveScience.* Live Science, 4 Mar. 2015. Web. 08 May 2017.

CHAPTER 7. A CHANGING CLIMATE

1. "Department of Finance Releases New State Population Projections." *Department of Finance.* Department of Finance, 8 Mar. 2017. Web. 19 Sept. 2017.

2. G. Dennis Cooke. *Restoration and Management of Lakes and Reservoirs.* Boca Raton, FL: CRC Press, 2005. Print. 5.

3. "Why Is Our Water in Trouble?" *Nature.org.* The Nature Conservancy, n.d. Web. 19 Sept. 2017.

4. "Study: Climate Change Rapidly Warming World's Lakes." *NASA.* NASA, 15 Dec. 2015. Web. 19 Sept. 2017.

5. Ibid.

6. "Climate Change: How Do We Know?" *NASA*. NASA, 15 May 2017. Web. 16 May 2017.

7. "Study: Climate Change Rapidly Warming World's Lakes." *NASA*. NASA, 15 Dec. 2015. Web. 19 Sept. 2017.

8. "Lake Ecosystem Critical to East African Food Supply Is Threatened by Climate Change." *ScienceDaily*. ScienceDaily, 20 Aug. 2003. Web. 19 Sept. 2017.

9. "Restoring a Disappearing Giant: Lake Chad." *World Bank*. The World Bank Group, 27 Mar. 2014. Web. 19 Sept. 2017.

10. Phil Williams. "Local View: Bonds, Water Authority's Efforts Spur Lake's Revival." *San Diego Union Tribune*. San Diego Union Tribune, 20 June 2010. Web. 19 Sept. 2017.

11. "Climate Change: How Do We Know?" *NASA*. NASA, 15 May 2017. Web. 16 May 2017.

12. Ibid.

13. Sarah Zielinski. "The Colorado River Runs Dry." *Smithsonian Magazine*. Smithsonian Institution, Oct. 2010. Web. 19 Sept. 2017.

14. Ibid.

CHAPTER 8. INVASIVE SPECIES

1. Dan Egan. *The Death and Life of the Great Lakes*. New York: W. W. Norton & Company, 2017. Print. xv–xvi.

2. Ibid. 120.

3. Ibid. 157.

4. "What We Do to Stop Ballast Water Introductions of Invasive Species." *National Wildlife Federation*. National Wildlife Federation, n.d. Web. 19 Sept. 2017.

5. "Sea Lamprey: A Great Lakes Invader." *Great Lakes Fishery Commission*. Great Lakes Fishery Commission, n.d. Web. 19 Sept. 2017.

6. Nicole Silk and Kristine Ciruna. *A Practitioner's Guide to Freshwater Biodiversity Conservation*. Washington, DC: Island Press, 2005. Print. 266.

7. "Frequently Asked Questions About Invasive Species." *Fish and Wildlife Service*. US Fish and Wildlife Service, n.d. Web. 19 Sept. 2017.

8. Dave Dempsey. *On the Brink: The Great Lakes in the 21st Century*. Lansing, MI: Michigan State UP, 2004. Print. 149.

9. Ibid.

CHAPTER 9. THE FUTURE OF LAKE CONSERVATION

1. Becky Striepe. "20 Ways to Conserve Water at Home." *Care 2*. Care 2, n.d. Web. 19 Sept. 2017.

2. Nicole Silk and Kristine Ciruna. *A Practitioner's Guide to Freshwater Biodiversity Conservation*. Washington, DC: Island Press, 2005. Print. 7.

3. "Endangered Species Act (ESA)." *NOAA Fisheries*. National Oceanic and Atmospheric Administration, n.d. Web. 19 Sept. 2017.

4. "Frequently Asked Questions about Mead/Bateson." *Intercultural Studies*. The Institute for Intercultural Studies, n.d. Web. 19 Sept. 2017.

INDEX

acid rain, 18, 19, 21, 64
agriculture, 12, 14, 18–19, 21, 23, 44–46, 48, 52, 63, 64, 69, 74, 75, 92
algae, 7, 8, 9, 12–13, 19, 22, 25, 67, 74, 76, 77
alligator gar, 36–38
aquifer, 14, 18, 52–53
Aral Sea, 48–50
Area of Concern, 11, 22
Asian carp, 37, 77, 85–86

best management practice, 21–22
biodiversity, 11, 12, 15, 23, 24, 27, 33, 34, 37, 39, 43, 58, 59, 61, 87, 97
biomagnification, 24
bottled water, 14, 50, 93
buffers, 22

canal, 48, 81–83, 86
Carson, Rachel, 24
Chad, Lake, 76–77
Chicago River, 7, 85
Clean Water Act, 9, 11, 89, 93

climate change, 13, 33, 49, 67–69, 73–77, 79, 90
Colorado River, 79
Core 4, 21–22
culvert, 61
Cuyahoga River, 5–7, 9, 11, 89

dam, 33, 38, 39, 48, 49, 53, 55–59, 61
deforestation, 19, 63–64, 67–69, 92
dredging, 27, 48, 79
drought, 46, 53, 69, 73, 74, 76, 79
dynamite, 34, 37

Edwards Dam, 59–60
Elsinore, Lake, 77, 79
Endangered Species Act, 93, 95
Environmental Protection Agency (EPA), 9, 22–23, 25, 27, 89
Erie, Lake, 7, 8–9, 11–13, 48, 83, 86
Erie Canal, 83

erosion, 19, 22
eutrophication, 19, 67
evaporation, 18, 44–46, 49, 70, 74, 77, 79
extinction, 15, 33, 34, 36, 38, 81, 93

fertilizer, 18, 19, 49
fishing, 8, 9, 11, 15, 18, 19, 33–34, 36–37, 39, 49
freshwater mussels, 24

Great Lakes, 7–8, 9, 34, 38–39, 83–87
Great Lakes Fisheries Commission, 87
Great Lakes Water Quality Agreement, 9
groundwater, 8, 14–15, 28, 49, 52–53, 70, 79

habitat loss, 33, 39, 97
health, 8, 12, 13, 24, 27, 38, 49, 67, 76
heat pollution, 44, 67, 74–75

industry, 6, 8, 14, 18, 22, 24–25, 27, 48–51, 75
International Union for Conservation of Nature (IUCN), 95
invasive species, 12, 22–23, 36, 38, 81–83, 85–87, 97
irrigation, 13, 18, 43, 44–46, 48, 51, 52, 53, 55, 79, 92

lake sturgeon, 38–39, 48, 58, 59, 61

mercury, 22, 25, 67
migration, 38, 55, 57, 58–61, 87
Muskegon Lake, 22–23

National Environmental Policy Act, 9
National Priorities List, 27
Nature Conservancy, 38, 69, 90, 92
NatureServe Network, 97
nonpoint source, 18
nutrients, 8, 12, 19, 21–22, 33, 55, 64, 67, 69, 76

overexploitation, 33–34, 36
Penobscot River, 59, 61
pesticide, 18, 21, 24, 49
phosphorus, 8, 9, 11, 12, 19, 25, 67
point source, 18
pollution, 6–7, 9, 12, 13, 15, 17–19, 21–25, 27, 28, 44, 49, 50, 56–57, 63–64, 77

quagga mussels, 12, 83, 85

reservoir, 18, 48, 52, 55, 57–58
restoration, 9, 15, 22, 38–39, 58–59, 69, 77, 79

Saint Lawrence Seaway, 83, 85
sea lamprey, 86–87
sediment, 18, 19, 21, 22, 25, 27, 55, 56–57, 63–64, 75, 79
sewage, 8, 11, 13, 17, 18, 24–25
spawning, 33, 38, 39, 48, 58, 64, 87, 90
Stryker Bay, 27
superfund site, 27

Tanganyika, Lake, 75–76
tillage, 21
Tonlé Sap Lake, 31, 33
tourism, 19, 92
trophic cascade, 40

Washington, Lake, 25
water cycle, 15, 70
water diversion, 43–46, 48–53, 79
water table, 53
watershed, 28, 61, 68, 77

zebra mussels, 12, 83, 85

ABOUT THE
AUTHOR

Lisa J. Amstutz is the author of many children's books and articles. She specializes in topics related to science, nature, and agriculture. Her background includes a BA in Biology and an MS in Environmental Science/Ecology. When Lisa isn't writing, you may find her tramping through the woods or curled up with a cup of tea and a good book.